"Goldberg's *Are we all postracial yet?* interrogates the idea of the postracial ... aspiration, but in fact the basis for a new phase of racial arrangements, shaped by shifts in the political economy, domestic and international law, and geopolitics. The work is theoretically rich and probing with both global and local implications. It deepens race critical theory, and furthers our understanding of the ongoing significance of race."

Imani Perry Hughes, Princeton University

"This book reveals the neo-raciality masked by the claims of the postracial. The underlying structures of economic, political, and social inequalities have seen the afterlife of racism in police uniforms walk the streets of America openly amidst the cries of 'I can't breathe' from its victims. A must read."

Ngũgĩ wa Thiong'o, University of California, Irvine

"Are we all postracial yet? David Theo Goldberg, in answering this question with a resounding 'yes,' explores the postracial as a logic and condition that enables racism to persist and proliferate. This book offers a sharp, wise, and unflinching critique of the racism of the postracial. It is also a deeply optimistic book: there is no better way of demanding an alternative than by demonstrating its necessity."

Sara Ahmed, Goldsmiths

"David Theo Goldberg's trenchant meditation on the challenges to anti-racist remediation reveals a structured cultural silence about deep social shape-shifting forms of inequality. The very term 'postracial' places racism's harms beyond critical analysis, rendered unreachable because located in the past, indecipherable because erased from language, and ungovernable because assigned to private rather than collective address. This excellent study explores the limits of 'postracialism' in an epoch of denial, unsparingly dissecting the common attributes of intersecting forms of prejudice."

Patricia Williams, Columbia Law School

"This pointed, thoughtful, and readable book is a bold intervention in the politics of undoing racial hierarchy. For too long, anti-racism has been inhibited by the difficulties involved in moving beyond critique. David Theo Goldberg has risen to the cosmopolitan challenge involved in breaking that logjam. With characteristic rigor and wit, he shows how anti-racist politics can be reconfigured in combative, practical, and affirmative forms."

Paul Gilroy, King's College London

Are we all postracial yet?

Are we all postracial yet?

DAVID THEO GOLDBERG

polity

First published in 2015 by Polity Press

Polity Press
65 Bridge Street
Cambridge CB2 1UR, UK

Polity Press
350 Main Street
Malden, MA 02148, USA

ISBN-13: 978-0-7456-8971-5
ISBN-13: 978-0-7456-8972-2 (pb)

A catalogue record for this book is available from the British Library.

Library of Congress Cataloging-in-Publication Data

Goldberg, David Theo.
   Are we all postracial yet? / David Theo Goldberg.
      pages cm
   Includes bibliographical references and index.
   ISBN 978-0-7456-8971-5 (hardback : alk. paper) – ISBN 978-0-7456-
8972-2 (pbk. : alk. paper)   1. Racism.   2. Race relations.
3. Anti-racism.   4. Multiculturalism.   I. Title.
   HT1521.G547 2015
   305.8–dc23

                                                                2015004085

Typeset in 11 on 15 pt Adobe Garamond
by Toppan Best-set Premedia Limited
Printed and bound in the USA by RR Donnelley

For further information on Polity, visit our website: politybooks.com for the folks on the bus

CONTENTS

I have been thinking about the postracial explicitly for some years now, at least since Barack Obama was first elected in November 2008. At the same time, my thinking about the racial, and the postracial in particular, has always exceeded any single nation-state experience. Any account of the anti-racial and the anti-racist today is also always about the postracial, if not explicitly named as such. My concern, it will quickly be seen, is not with how exasperatingly far we are from postraciality, conventionally understood, even in the face of its insistence. Rather, it is to make sense of how racisms can proliferate, can be so crudely persistent and obvious, in the face of their equally insistent claims to be over, socially irrelevant, no longer of real concern. This is the knot I shall address in this little book. I will be at pains to describe in some detail the threads constituting the knot, how they came to emerge historically, their sociologics and force, their renewed subjects of expression and targets. I will suggest in conclusion ways of thinking about their critical address. The driving question is how racist expression can thrive at the very moment that racial configuration is claimed to be a thing of the past.

Although I have been thinking for a good while about these issues, the book itself was written very quickly. I was approached by Polity late in 2013 to consider writing a short book on the subject for the new series "Debating Race." By the time things had been worked out, March had rolled by and the book's delivery date was six months away. I was in the midst of co-organizing what would come to be a remarkable event in July 2014. The University of California Humanities Research Institute (UCHRI), which I direct, has been convening two-week summer institutes in different global sites, the Seminar in Experimental Critical Theory, for a decade now. The Johannesburg Workshop in Theory and Criticism (JWTC) has been running a comparable workshop each July since 2009, with which I have also been engaged since its inception. We happily combined our resources to run a mobile workshop for two weeks across South Africa, fortuitously for the writing of this book, on "the archives of the nonracial." I sat down to write the manuscript on the flight home from South Africa in mid-July. For better and worse, three intensive months later I delivered the manuscript. Sometimes the gods of intellectual production oblige.

The South African workshop was designed to engage key historical sites of anti-apartheid struggle across

South Africa in addressing theoretical and global issues of race, racism, and the nonracial. The undertaking was to drive almost sixty intellectuals, artists, and activists from across the world around South Africa for two weeks to engage with each other as well as with local interlocutors at each of our stopping points in the interests of animating a sustained project of thinking (about) the nonracial. We started in Johannesburg, wound our way up to Mbabane in Swaziland, site of a significant anti-apartheid exile gathering, then drove down to Durban, on to Qunu, Transkei, overlooking Nelson Mandela's birth and resting places, and then to the Biko Centre for Black Consciousness in Ginsburg, King William's Town. We ended our remarkable journey in Cape Town. It was co-organized with my dear friends and colleagues Achille Mbembe, Kelly Gillespie, Leigh-Ann Naidoo, Zen Marie, Julia Hornberger, and Annie (Dhammamega) Leatt. The thinking of this book is deeply marked by this extraordinary experience and set of intensely generative engagements. No one on the bus was left unmarked by the interaction. I should stress, though, that no one but me is accountable for any assertion or argument appearing in these pages.

I want to thank all of the bus people for an extraordinarily rich experience. It is to them and all they stood for in living the values of the critical nonracial that I dedicate this book. As the names to be rehearsed are too numerous, I restrict myself to those with whom direct interactions on and off the bus, and before and after the trip, impacted the way I may have thought about issues pertinent to the book. My co-organizers especially, both leading up to and extending beyond the workshop, had a profound charge on the argument, most notably, though not only, Achille and Kelly. A special shout-out also goes to Commandante Leigh-Ann, without whose vision and extraordinary organizational talents the bus would not have departed Johannesburg. The road allowed me to extend long-standing impactful critical conversations with dear friends Angela Davis, Gina Dent, Ghassan Hage, Ruha Benjamin, Sarah Nuttall, as well as Siba Grovongui, Francoise Verges, Michael Keith, Xolela Mangcu, Nisha Kapoor, and the inimitable (in their own ways) Neo Muyanga and Roberta Estrella d'Alva. New lines of engagement were initiated with Mark Matera, Ainehi Edoro, Azeen Khan, and Eric Reinhard.

Three events helped to reshape the manuscript as I was revising it. One was a follow-up workshop at UCHRI with Achille and Kelly, among others. Another, organized by Dilip Gaonkar at Northwestern University, took place as protests were breaking out in the wake of the grand jury decisions not to prosecute the police in the killings of Michael Brown and Eric Garner. My thinking was renewed by both. The public conversation that Helena Chavez organized with dear friends John and Jean Comaroff (family really), Cuahtemoc Medina, and Federico Navarette at MUAC (the Museum of Contemporary Art) in Mexico City helped me clarify central points.

The gods of intellectual production include some very real people, in addition to those already named. I could not have done this without the support of the extraordinary staff of UCHRI. It is hard to say that administrative responsibility is a pleasure, especially when it so proliferates in and constrains academic life. And yet my colleagues at the Institute make it seem so, seamlessly ensuring that my distraction would leave no mark on the daily routine of institutional life. This book would not have been possible without their collective support, not to mention their interest in the work itself. I am grateful to Anna Finn for her careful research, editorial, and indexing contributions.

Over the past few years I have been in extended conversation about social and political theory, theories of race and racism with Diren Valayden as he completed his remarkable dissertation, "Outbreak Racism: The Embrace of Risk after Structural Racism," at the

University of California, Irvine. The influence of Diren's thinking and work in opening up a line of analysis about new forms of racist expression will be evident in the pages that follow. Likewise with my dear friends Ackbar Abbas, Saree Makdisi, and Jenna Ng, who commented critically on bits and pieces of the argument and writing along the way. Susan Searls Giroux pushed me early on in my thinking about postraciality. A conversation with Fakhry Davids over a dinner in London late in the process impacted some revision.

The people of Polity Press have again been a delight to work with. The series editors, first Emma Longstaff and then Jonathan Skerrett, shepherded the book effortlessly through the process with thoughtful advice. The efforts of production editor Clare Ansell and tireless copy-editor Justin Dyer resulted in a much improved manuscript. David Roediger kindly reviewed the initial draft for the press, and his insightful suggestions likewise made for a considerably better book.

No one has more readily and lastingly affected my way of thinking than Philomena Essed. Daily conversations and interactions around matters of race and so much else continue to exemplify what it means to live without the color line even while living very much in a world marked by it.

ONE

The pasts of the postracial

Race today is supposed to be a thing of the past. And yet all we do, seemingly, is to talk about it. We talk (about) race when not talking (about) it; and we don't talk (about) it when (we should be) talking (about) it. "The postracial," as filmmaker Michael Oblowitz recently put it to me with his characteristic rap-rhetoricality, "is the most racial." Such is the condition, the paradox, of postraciality.

A postracial paradox

The postracial is all about us. It was born – or in a sense raciality was born again, anew – when Barack Obama got elected in 2008. With America's first black President, postraciality went public, pronouncing itself the prevailing state of being, at least aspirationally. This quickly opened up a frenzied media discussion about whether America, in particular, and other once racially predicated societies globally, had become postracial. It seems that all it takes for a (once) self-proclaimed white country's racial history to be wiped clean is for a black man-hero – an Obama or Mandela – to get elected President. The Great Man version of history takes a new turn on stage.

The claim that we today inhabit – or have come close(r) to inhabiting – a postracial society embeds the insistence that key conditions of social life are less and less now predicated on racial preferences, choices, and resources. These include residential location, educational possibility and institutional access, employment opportunities, social networks and interaction – in short, life's chances overall. Postraciality amounts to the claim that we are, or are close to, or ought to be living outside of debilitating racial reference. In particular, it presumes that people (ought to) have similar life chances irrespective of their assigned race in societies such as the United States and South Africa. It presumes that effort, energy, and inherent ability will determine individuals' life prospects. It insists that the legacy of racial discrimination and disadvantage has been waning over time, reaching a point today where, if existing at all, such discrimination is anomalous and individually expressed. It is not structural or socially mandated. Postracial racial outbursts – the awkwardness of the characterization itself revealing of their anomaly – are taken to be occasional not systemic or systematic, with diminishing impact. They are supposedly to be treated like curses on the road: roll up the window and drive on by.

Postraciality, accordingly, is both assertion and aspiration (Steele 2008; Hollinger 2011). It is both descriptive or factual and normative. Why, then, the popularity of the "postracial" now, not just in America but pretty much wherever race has (had) significant resonance? The argument that follows in this book offers one line of under-remarked response to this pressing question.

As with racialities and racisms generally, postracial conditions and articulations will differ across societies, given their contrasting racial histories. There is a notable contrast between the explicit, if sometimes banal, discussions in the United States regarding the realization of postraciality, the sometime aspirational expression in South Africa, and the virtual silence about the postracial in Brazil.

So why has public racist expression generally become far more virile and vicious in the name of the postracial than it has been since the 1960s? Examples abound: in the United States, widespread racially charged comments about Obama, the killings of Trayvon Martin in Sanford, Florida, Michael Brown in Ferguson, Missouri, and Eric Garner in New York, discussions about police brutality and about Dreamers; across Europe, the connected resurgence of anti-Semitism, Islamophobia, and anti-immigration sentiment; in Israel, the explosion of explicitly racist sensibilities regarding both Palestinians and African migrants. What (and who), in the face of this reality, is the postracial actually for? And again, what racial work is the postracial doing, what racist expression is it enabling, legitimating, rationalizing? Is it just, as Lipsitz (2012: 1) argues, that postraciality was "created to mask the effects of white privilege"?

It's not that there has been no "progress" on racial matters. We can all point to the visible markers of formal and experiential shifts: 1954, 1964, and 1965, and again 2008 in the United States; 1990 and 1994 in South Africa; and so on. But progress in some areas, even importantly the election of the first black President, doesn't preclude regression or extended and new forms of racist expression in others. Racism here means the curtailment of life and life's prospects, of social standing and rights, of personal dignity and social possibility because of one's perceived race. The question is whether these new and renewed racist expressions are stand-alone events, anomalies, or part of a larger emergent pattern, a novel structure of raciological articulation. I will be arguing that they are definitively the latter.

Postraciality, it could be said, then, is the end of race as we have known it.

Before Fox News runs with this as its headline, now confirmed by an academic critic they would love to hate, note what this does not say. It emphatically does not declare that race, let alone racism, has reached its end. Dinesh D'Souza (1996) and others have continued to arrogate that untenable claim even while awkwardly advancing its contrary in film and print so as to dismiss Barack Obama as driven by anti-colonial commitments (D'Souza 2011; Scott 2014). Similarly, conservative commentator John McWhorter (2008) insisted immediately following Obama's election that "Racism is over.... It is not a moral duty to keep it front and center." He added two years later that "Obama's first year has shown us again and again that race does not matter in America in the way it used to. We've come more than a mere long way – we're almost there" (McWhorter 2010). Shelby Steele (2007) initially predicted Obama's unelectability to the Presidency. Confronted by the electoral counter-factual in November 2008, he unapologetically dismissed it as the racially charged victory of America's hollowed-out civil rights legacy (Steele 2008). Driven by white guilt, Obama's election supposedly wasn't postracial enough!

What the claim about postraciality as the end of race suggests, rather, is simply that a certain way of thinking about race, and implicitly of racist expression, has been giving way to novel understandings, orders, and arrangements of racial designation and racist expression. Race (as we have known it) may be over. But racism lives on unmarked, even unrecognized, potentially for ever.

Racisms across history

Race swept across the worlds of modernity, making and unmaking states and societies in its terms. Racial articulation and configuration have shaped modern worlds in ways proving challenging, if not impossible to undo as the modern gives way to its various "post"-formations and formulations. As a dominating mode of command throughout modernity, race has ordered the prevailing definitions and structures of the social, the state, and its subjects. Indeed, the enduring conditions made and marked by the racial continue to structure society. This is so regardless of the fact that its various explicit manifestations may now be rejected, rendered implicit, silenced, or denied. Racism has been declared over, an antique relic, and a banal state of the postracial is deemed now to pervade.

How is it that race has so broadly impacted modern lifeworlds, its remains still reverberating (Amin 2010), still proving so commanding and intractable even in its afterlife, its eruptions still haunting? Race materialized as an expression of "dehumanization" as the geography of modern Europe took form. Race established the lines of belonging and estrangement for modern European social life. This "racialization," as Fanon (1968) would later characterize the mode of dehumanizing at work in the name of race, was fashioned and elaborated as the modern idea of Europe was shaped from the Renaissance onwards. Race was invoked to delineate a European "we" in defining contrast with those considered its constitutive outsiders: not just Jews and Muslims subjected to conversion and expulsion, but blacks too. This, then, constitutes the haunting trinity of non-belonging shadowing Europe's founding at the onset of European globalization (Goldberg 2002).

So racial configuration is knotted from the outset of its formulation and social fashioning with religious resonance: Jews and Muslims, black and Indian heathens as Europe's formative non-belonging. Differentiating origins, kinship, and lineage from the outset tied color to culture, bodies to behavioral projections, incipient biology to ascribed mentalities. And as race, in its ever-morphing and cementing significance, was adopted increasingly as a central technology of modern state constitution and reason, it assumed its defining power by absorbing some of the remaining theological resonances it is taken to have displaced.

Once the purview of the religious, these defining features became racial. They included the narrative of human origins; the passion and force of kinship commitment; and the naturalizing of the artifice of socially produced and fashioned identifications. As religion did for the medieval, race now offered for modernity the imagining of mass community out of individualized social anonymity. Indeed, race projected a sense of generalized population – a society – from a narrow base of immediately familial or communal experience. Race now shaped romanticized belonging, sanctified exclusion and expulsion, and legitimated death as religion had done. And as race became the object of critical accounts rather than taken up as primarily productive of sociality, like religion it was dismissed as socially antique, a hold-over from the pre-modern, as socially regressive.

Race, in short, is *the secularization of the religious*. It abstractly pulled more or less silently into its own terms of articulation the technologies and expressions of religion's productive socialities. Race made these conditions modern in much the way that religion expressed the medieval and pre-modern past. Race took on religious resonance both in the fervor of its expressed commitments and in its shaping of belonging and preclusion.

The racial is secularized, then, in two related, modernizing ways: first, it increasingly is made a governing technology in modern state formation; and, second, racial identification is elaborated through formalized classification schemes establishing population hierarchies. Where once such social standing or lack was established through religious determination, racial definition assumed the leading articulation for modern social orders and state formations. I demonstrate in Chapter 4 how this secularization of the religious manifests itself today in the contemporary management of Muslims and the proliferation of Muslimania.

The broad historical arc of racial thinking and institutionalization marks all of modernity. From the fifteenth to the nineteenth centuries, slavery framed much if not all the thinking concerning race. Slavery was fueled by ideas of inherent inferiority and superiority, and reinforced them. Racial ideas have always been diverse, shifting over time, even throughout slavery. New World Indians were socially understood and treated differently than Old World Africans. Both were enslaved, though the latter somewhat more readily than

9

the former, if the Spanish state is an indication here. Jews and Moors were held under suspicion as subverting the truth of the Testament, forced into conversion and expulsion on pain of torturous death. Chinese and Batavians, Japanese and Indians were pressed into household service and in time more readily became the media of miscegenated family life.

Race thus has massaged boundaries and strictures, restrictions and possibilities in and across these life-worlds. It drove and structured both globalization and local space, mapping the contours of belonging, opportunity, and limit. The racial, in short, has always exhibited this oddly contradictory sense, pulling in different directions. It fixes people in place, setting them within the bounds and constraints of pre-conceived notions of nature, possibility, and presumptuous predictability. At the same time, race represented a socio-conceptual agility, a signifying promiscuity, in pinning down people and societies while at once evading being cemented to singularly given meaning, significance, and value.

This, then, has been the enduring utility of raciality for modernity. Its conceptual promiscuity and lability have shaped populations, ordering opportunities for some while curtailing them for others, enabling the exercise of power and subjection. This racial elasticity has also offered the social capacity to re-order the social, to renew modes of social control, aggrandizing some while relationally diminishing others. This lack of racial fixity has served the interests of power well by enabling an agile capacity to cement people in place. It has homogenized the heterogeneous, a key tool of modernizing social management.

States accordingly assumed modernity through the governing technologies of race. Race drove colonizing formations while also defining the metropolis in relation to them. It marked social standing and access, privilege and power. It initially defined who was human and who was not, who belonged and who was exploitable, not only who could work but the kind of work they were licensed to do. Race identified whose bodies were alienable, who counted socially and who were disposable, who were fit to live (on) and who could be left or made to die, where and how.

The prevailing definition of racial conception from the fifteenth to the nineteenth centuries ordained those of European descent as inherently superior, and non-Europeans or those regarded less fully European as ranking on a scale of ontological inferiority and objectification. It thus naturalized the outcomes of political and economic power struggles, fixing them in place. This racial naturalism underpinned slavery as well as other forms of violent annihilative state action, from Spanish colonialism, the Belgian Free State, and German South West Africa to Nazi Germany. (It seems that any state nominating itself "Free" does so by driving the indigenous and non-belonging into laboring and sexual servitude, invisibility, and what Ruth Wilson Gilmore [2007] calls the "premature death" produced by racism.)

Since modernity's onset, then, race has offered variable modes of social ordering, state arrangement, and interpersonal relation. It made and marked pretty much every meaningful condition of social standing and access across life's prospects and death's likelihood. Race articulated with the registers of class and gender to reify possibility, standardize lifeworlds and life-ways, and reproduce both conditions and horizons of life- and death-ways, literally from pre-natality to post-mortem, birth right to burial site.

Racisms have always presupposed population definition, conditions of distantiation, and disposability: the "Negro" or "Black," the Muslim or "Moor," the "Jew," the "Asiatic" or "Oriental," and so also, if more implicitly or implicatively, the "White" or "Caucasian," or "European." These are racially configured identifications. Their imposition and adoption arose from the interplay of scientific and popular discourses, philosophical and religious definition, literary and historical representation, political and cultural classification. They have thus also always been about both geography and spatiality, about geopolitical order at the macro scale and local design and lived arrangements at the more micro levels.

At the micro-local register, the racially produced tensions born of refusing relation with the different, of promoting interactive avoidance, and denying social heterogeneity fuel immediately targeted aggressions. These sometimes have deadly consequences. They mirror and multiply the abstractions of macro-racial expression. Here racisms, more or less deadly in their outbursts and extended effects, not infrequently violent in their expression, are the immediate expressions of longer conflictual histories. The ethnocentric assumes the "modernizing" tenor and terror of raciological eruption. When racial characterization is added to the mix, the hostile and volatile can quickly be rendered explosive.

So, racisms and their expressions are to a larger or lesser degree concerned with defining, deploying, and disposing of people and their products. They establish who controls those modes of consideration and activation. In short, racisms are about the control of power: who gets to exercise and suffer its enactment.

Counter-racial conceptions

Now a counter-conception of racial articulation was at work from at least the sixteenth century, pushing back against naturalizing domination without (a)voiding racial commitment. One could call this the first anti-racism. In so doing it sets in motion the series of historical counter-racisms and responses going forward. This initial counter- or anti-racism was first expressed by the likes of Las Casas in the debate with Sepulveda in the 1550s, in ways that began to make evident the role of the state in racial determination. This initiating counter-tradition of the racial found non-European human groups not to be *inherently* inferior. So the first, perhaps most obvious, expression of anti-racism, in both historical and conceptual form, could be marked in terms of its anti-naturalizing commitment.

This anti-naturalizing commitment reveals as much about prevailing modes of racial refusal ever since as it does about the racisms it takes itself to be resisting. It insisted, generally, that those not European were to be hierarchically ranked as less historically mature, less historically civilized, than those delineated European or Euro-derivative, as Euro-provincials. Here, nothing inherently prevents any non-European from advancing (through education and self-striving) to maturity.

Non-Europeans accordingly could acquire civilization, could become civilized (effectively by mimicking the European in education, culture, and habits). Becoming civilized equaled advancing in the exercise of rational capacity. The fact that "Non-European" became with time an emphatic racial designation, and at one point an administrative state category, reveals the racial logic implicit here.

What I have elsewhere designated *racial historicism* (Goldberg 2002), then, embeds a humanism. It implies a humanizing possibility, even as it denies immediately existing equality across all registers of existence and social standing. This racial historicism fueled much of the abolitionist movement, including some prominent black activists like Edward Blyden, and was principally identified with John Stuart Mill in both his philosophical writing and administrative colonial function. It underpins a wide range of representations and policies from the eighteenth to the twentieth centuries: from Latin American *Casta* paintings to policies of *blanqueamiento* and racial democracy, Anglo-assertion in India and South Africa, and French colonial assimilationism.

In the hundred and fifty years following abolition in the United States, administrative policy and social management regarding diverse state populations remained

racially configured, though racially articulated administration of state population, spatial arrangement,
and national identity shifted over time. These shifts,
more or less every two decades, reflected changing political and demographic conditions, transforming relations and sentiment, tastes and dispositions, both at
home and more globally. Shifts can be discerned from
the nineteenth century, across the long twentieth
century, and into the new millennium: from *reconstruction* to *segregation*, *assimilation* to *integration* and *colorblindness* (or *racelessness* more broadly). Integration,
in turn, gave way to and got incorporated into *multiculturalism* following the civil rights movement and
Vietnam War.

Multiculturalism emerged as a cultural and policy
response to the resulting diversities. It was driven in part
by increased late- and post-colonial immigration from
the global South to the North, heightened by the global
recession of the mid-1970s and the reach for greater
economic opportunity.

One can find similar trajectories in the cases of Australia and Canada. In Latin America, post-abolition
gave way to policies of *blanquiamiento*, racial democracy, multiculturalism, and more recently the rise
of a modestly reparative justice policy embedded
in affirmative action access to higher education. In

Europe, eugenicism gave way largely to postwar racial skepticism (as in referential racial avoidance) and half-hearted multiculturalisms.

Each of these designations marked a racial conception both breaking with and incorporating earlier ones. They suggest novel ways of understanding while reinstating racial conditions and policy implementation around population formation and their technologies of management, discipline, and control.

Slavery obviously delimited basic rights: the right (to the right) to life, liberty, property, political expression (principally through voting), and associating for political purpose. These restrictions to a greater or lesser degree affected also those blacks and populations of color more generally who were not enslaved. Post-abolition reconstruction initially committed, however modestly, to extend to black people's voting rights, political representation, limited land, and technologies of production. (In the United States, the offer of "forty acres and a mule" was originally considered for freed slaves in and immediately following the Civil War. More often than not, however, they ended up as share-croppers and unskilled labor working for no more than subsistence wages.

By contrast, in many cases (including Britain and America), the state moved to pay not insignificant compensation to slave owners for their eroded wealth in discounting their chattel property. It seems that reparations for suffering racial injustice have repeatedly been offset if not thoroughly outstripped by "reparations" for wealth deemed lost and forgone as a result of ending the perpetrated injustice. Such payments both presupposed and extended rather than challenged the presumption that slaves counted as slave-holders' property. Tort welfare for whites long pre-dated the welfare state.

Emancipation formally enabled liberated slaves to live where their means enabled them. Yet as racial devaluation continued to discount black (and more broadly non-white, non-European) lives and their contributions, the political power of white privilege sought ways to restrict black mobility and choices. Such restrictions operated across the registers of civic, economic, and political life. Segregation is the totalizing set of structural conditions by which these restrictions on generalized mobility, access, and possibility became known. It was the extension of racially inscribed power and privilege, the object and outcome of necessarily renewed anti-racist and anti-racial resistance. Segregation was ensured through a mix of formal technologies like law and policy formation and informal economic means such as pricing racial undesirables out of the market.

The most immediate declarative counter to the separating logics of segregation arguably was *assimilation*. Where the logics of segregation were to set apart, the assimilative conceptual logic was to pull individuals from once excluded groups into the "melting pot" of prevailing political arrangements and structures. It sought to provide the non-belonging the opportunity to acculturate by melting into and operating on the common logics defined by dominant – namely white – interests. Those not racially dominant (not white) could become white-like by adopting their values, habits, cultural expressions, aspirations, and ways of being. Assimilationism is an anti-racialism, or at least a nominal nonracialism, in the interests of pulling the racially excluded into the polity of already well-established definition and possibility. As Steve Biko (1978: 24) once commented, assimilationism changes nothing of the underlying structures of inequality, economically and politically, leaving the "set of norms and code of behavior, the values and structures determining privilege and power already established self-servingly by whites firmly in place." The values of exclusion, the metrics of unequal exchange, become the grounds of assimilative encounter. The nonracial is predicated on the givens of pre-established racialities now embedded (almost) silently into the polity.

19

Assimilation forces competition and access on the basis of structures and rules already favoring the long-established racially privileged and powerful. It naturalizes the histories of elevation and devaluation into the presupposed neutrality of the claim to the now nonracial. By contrast, *integration* seeks to open up to contestation norms, rules of engagement, and values of assessment. If the aim is to engage as equals, the terms of engagement must be structured to conjure confidence in their fairness. Integration gestures at the ground rules for such a negotiation. It assumes, somewhat naïvely, that if the procedures are fair, the outcomes must be just (think here of Rawls), no matter that deep existing imbalances in power and possibility will materially affect inputs and outputs in the negotiable exchange.

As with assimilation, integration is more at ease with what I will call, enigmatically, a *racial nonracialism* than with anti-racisms. Racial nonracialism seeks to sidestep historical legacies of racial arrangement and injustice. Anti-racism, by contrast, seeks to critically address and redress the impacts of those legacies. Racial nonracialism takes up race more or less explicitly not to identify and address racially produced historical inequalities and inequities, more or less irreparable violent harms and their cumulative effects. It takes up race much more modestly to identify those excluded so as to bring them into the fold of a society no longer seen as racially unjust. The historical injustices recognized by such nonracialism are not the extended losses brought into the present from that history, the remainders of race, so much as the superficiality of not being assimilated or integrated. The racial here simply marks the absence of nonraciality as opposed to racial equality in the production and reproduction of the nation-state. Rather than being produced through thoughtful public policy, assimilationist or integrationist nonraciality, where it occurs at all, is just happy happenstance.

Colorblindness, in turn, takes as its register the color to which it purports to be blind. It sees race while asserting a blindness to that which it must see to express the disavowal. This is seeing through race in the sense both of seeing the world framed by race and of recognizing the pitfalls, limits, privileges, and burdens such frames enable and produce (Mitchell 2012). Racial nonracialism, epistemologically, is knowingly ignorant and, in political terms, committedly non-committal. A special kind of perverse double consciousness.

This perverse double consciousness – of the racial while blind to it – became the prevailing normative commitment, at least rhetorically, in societies such as the United States that had become marked by the recognition of rapidly expanding multi-raciality. The *racial nonraciality* of multi-racialism squeezes itself into the presupposed moderate middle ground animated in the growing romance with mixed race and hybridity. Squeezed between the projected binary extremes of two racialities – white against black – the multi- and the middle, the mixed and hybrid assume the romanticized value of "all getting along." *Institutional multiculturalism* effectively became, from the 1970s to the new millennium, this naming of the *racially* unnameable. Where the *nonracial* – the negation or distinctive denial – mutes the racial, raciality mutates into multiculturalism.

Now, race and ethnicity have long, even constitutively, overlapped. They intersect, defining each other at least in part. Following World War II, especially in the European theatre, ethnicity came to define the principal demographic distinction in the wake of raciality's projected evaporation. Considered less divisive and less socially dangerous, ethno-cultural characterization was invoked to parse population belonging, draw boundaries, and (more or less quietly) close borders and order banishment. It served to shape, define, and contain the mobilities that always have exceeded the terms of controlling constraint. The silencing of race came to be filled by more consumable cultural proliferation. Race and ethnicity once again amalgamated through the registers of culture.

Ironically, however, this celebration of cultural multiplicity overlooks the extended culturizing of the racial, its repetitive expression through cultural distinction. Whites, stereotypically, have taken themselves throughout modernity to be hard-working, blacks to be criminally lazy, Muslims to be violent, Asians to be inscrutable. This culturalization is, in short, a stepping-stone to racialities' "post-al" reach, their ghostly afterlife. Ethno-raciality became the new raciality in the name of what from 1970 on came to be called multiculturalism. The new "black," I am tempted to say, with a wink and a nod, is not so far from its departed predecessor. As "orange became the new black," the "new black" was just the old "black" now in orange garb. (After all, these developments coincided with the rapidly spiraling black and brown prison population from the early 1970s to the end of the millennium.)

This genealogy of racialities and nonracialities played itself out, exhausted and bankrupted, by the first decade of the new millennium. The dance with multiculturalism lasted all of a quarter-century, trailing off at the twentieth century's end and the start-up culture of the new millennium. British Prime Minister David

Cameron, backed up by German Chancellor Angela Merkel, declared "war on (state) multiculturalism," blaming it for fomenting "extremist ideologies" and "home-grown Islamic terrorism."

The postracial present

The postracial, then, emerged as the cringe factor to multiculturalism's perceived or projected excesses and failures. In the latter's wake, postraciality asserts itself as the end of race, as we have known it, the assertive expression of what Cameron, in the same breath as he killed off multicultural policy, called a "muscular liberalism." Far from being the end of racisms, then, postraciality represents rather a certain way of thinking about race, and implicitly of racist expression. Raciality has been giving way to novel understandings, orders, and arrangements, as Cameron's language implies. The postracial, in short, far from being the end of race, is a neo-raciality, racisms' extension if not resurrection. It is, one could say, the implication if not effect of racial historicism, its predictable outcome, only now with vehemently exclusionary import. The religiously extreme and violent can only be saved from themselves, and the rest of us can only be saved from them, by purging them through intellectual "maturation" of their misguided multicultural ways.

The following chapters take up, in turn, what it is that constitutes the racial "conditions" of the postracial, what the notion stands for; its racio-logics of operation and technologies of social governance; the figuring of the postracial subject, who is to be considered the characteristic contemporary target of the postracial; and finally what futures after racisms might critically amount to.

Postracial conditions

I argued at the close of Chapter 1 that the postracial (as claim, as interest) emerges in the form of exhaustion with and rejection of multicultural policy. The "post" in the "postracial" is the reversal of, the push back against, the "multi-" of the "cultural." The postracial is the antibody to multiculturality, and in its more extreme expressions even to cultural multiplicity and demographic diversity. In the United States, the reaction against immigration, against integrated neighborhoods and schools, the whitewashing in parts of the country of school history textbooks, the call to "close borders" against Ebola or immigrants, are all indicative of the resistance to expansive diversity, demographically and culturally.

This sensibility abounds also in the insistence by the Israeli government that Israel is and must at all costs remain "a Jewish state." As an exclusively Jewish state, with some rights reserved to Jewish citizens not available to non-Jews, Israel accordingly is not a multicultural society. It is often identified by extension as

European, and so white, amidst the antagonisms of the surrounding Muslim-Arab and now African threat. This sentiment was readily revealed in then Interior Minister Eli Yishai's (2012) projection that Muslims forcefully "deny that the country belongs to us, to the white man" (an ironic assertion, given Yishai's Moroccan background). This collapses the racial with the religious, the cultural with the theological (Bear 2012).

Key elements of postracial conception were already implicit in the very comprehension of liberalism and its historical reiterations: the stress on the individual, the moral and political refusal of racial reference, predicated on the denial of group relevance as well as historical disparities in wealth and power. When these elements reinforce each other, as they did increasingly from the late 1990s onwards, racial liberalism as then embedded in multicultural policy started giving way to expanding neoliberal postraciality. At heart, postraciality is anti-multicultural, as both social arrangement and normative value.

Racial experience and structure

Neoliberalism's increasing stress on individualizing self-responsibility – on caring for oneself, on self-enterprise

27

and self-creation as the driving conditions of responsible self-direction – encourages an exploding impatience with group or communal claims. The spiraling skepticism towards multiculturalism resulted in its ultimate political dismissal, especially by national leaders David Cameron and Angela Merkel, among others. This goes hand in glove with the rising stress on postracial individualization and the renewed emphasis on nationalist discourses.

Renewed nationalisms are taken up in part as the forums for expansive commodification: flag and anthemic culture sells goods from clothing and cosmetics to sports tickets, tourist packages, automobiles, and technology. But nationalisms also contribute the cohering condition for otherwise isolated individualisms. "[I]t doesn't make any difference if you're Hispanic, or you're white, or you're Asian, or you're black, "urged US Republican Congressman Mo Brooks, "people throughout America want to do what's in the best interest of America" (Levine 2014). There may be no such thing as society for libertarians, as Thatcher famously put it, but the battle-cry of the nation serves as the compelling surrogate. War, which was once financed by the selling of national bonds, now reinforces social commitment while its designs supply the next cool technology for all to consume.

Ghassan Hage (2014) helpfully recalls a longstanding distinction in racist articulation between exploitation and extermination. Exploitative racisms work to extract identified value. This is usually productive labor, though it can also take the form of additional charges (a "racial tax") for those racially marginalized if close to hand. Eliminationist racisms serve to exclude completely from the national or neighborhood space those considered without value, if not to exterminate them. Exploitative racisms marginalize the racially othered *within* society, to use Hage's terms. Eliminationist racisms, by contrast, seek to distance or alienate – to excise – the racially differentiated *from* the nation-state. The means are various: deportation, offshoring, cleansing, or destruction, killing or letting die, to invoke Foucault's (2003) distinction. Always extreme, eliminationist means include extermination without being limited to it. Often, the eliminationist and exploitative operate interactively: apartheid sought to eliminate blacks from "white space" in order to heighten their exploitative potential by intensifying competition among unskilled labor.

Today one could add a third rail of racist articulation, one veering between the exploitative and the exterminating. Postraciality heightens the mode of racial *dismissal*. Dismissal ties together in its racial elaboration the disposition of ignoring with that of ignorance, indignity with humiliation. It hides group dismissal in the shadows of individuated assessment, rendering the former more difficult, even impossible, to discern. Racial dismissal trades on the dual logic of reversal. It charges the historically dispossessed as the now principal perpetrators of racism, while dismissing as inconsequential and trivial the racisms experienced by the historical targets of racism. In doing so, racial dismissal renders opaque the structures making possible and silently perpetuating racially ordered power and privilege. It reduces responsibility for degradation and disprivilege to individuated inexperience, lack of effort and incapacity, bad judgment, and ill fortune.

In thinking about racial conditions historically and contemporarily, then, it remains important to distinguish analytically between the *experiential* and the *structural*.

Historically, racial arrangements have *structured* societies to establish or extend as well as privilege the power of some racially defined over those differentially designated and socially positioned. The set of structural conditions identified with racial power and privilege is invariably marked as "whiteness" (Ahmed 2014b); that of relational and relative structural disprivilege and powerlessness as "blackness." Since their earliest manifestation, those racial designators of privilege, power, and their lack have been complexly articulated with religion, as I indicated in Chapter 1. And as many have demonstrated, they are intersectional with other modes of social positioning, privileging, empowering, and exclusion, most notably class and gender. Historically, where, say, Jews and Muslims have been racially conceived and marked, it has invariably been in the figures of blackness and brownness, of non-whiteness, or non-European as non-white.

People *experience* racially marked or charged events and conditions differently. Obviously this will turn on how one is racially marked in and by a society, but it also depends on one's social standing relative to such racial marking. Racial experience accordingly will be affected by less visible structural conditions regarding race.

Experiential racism – the personal and collective experience of racist expression or action – will be a function, then, of underlying structural conditions, more or less directly. When routinized, as they more or less are across modern societies, such experiences in turn reinforce the racial structures already shaping the social. Daria Roithmayr (2014: 4–10) demonstrates how individual choices by the already racially privileged reinforce and reproduce existing structural inequalities.

Referring a friend to a job, being economically positioned to help one's child with college tuition or college preparation lessons, "lock in" advantages that persist across lives, lifetimes, even generations.

Nonracial and anti-racist commitments likewise assume – as they must if they are to be effective – the intersecting forms of the experiential and the structural. The choice will turn on what sort of society is being sought, and the most effective ways to bring it about. It will turn, however, also on how racism is understood, and how best to confront its various forms and expressions: whether to avoid, evade, or resist.

If Jim Crow and apartheid segregation unarguably institutionalized structural racisms, they in turn impacted (as they were impacted by) experiential forms of racist expression. Structural racisms deliver or position subjects for racially discriminatory treatment. They license those with the power to discriminate and abuse while devaluing those positioned as their targets, reducing them from persons to mere objects, from self-determining subjects to nothing more than things or animals. Squeezed between slavery and segregation, reconstruction likewise sought overwhelmingly to address the structural conditions underpinning extended discriminatory impacts, with experiential effect. Reconstruction undertook, at least nominally, to expand political representation, modestly to redistribute land, and to open some opportunities to emancipated slaves and their families. Reconstruction, then, was first and foremost a structural anti-racism.

Integration is the undertaking, at least in conception, to enable all social members to enjoy equal rights, educational and economic opportunities, and desegregated residential conditions. It can be understood in structural terms, too. Assimilationism and multiculturalism, by contrast, both overwhelmingly resonated experientially. The structural transformations they each enacted were dramatically delimited, at best. Integration was conceived with political and economic transformation in mind. Affirmative action or "positive discrimination" as instruments of integration were intended, if in limited ways, to open educational and employment opportunities for historically restricted population groups, those deeply marked by "disparate impacts" of social practices. That they were so quickly and vocally resisted is testament to their at least structurally transformative potential, threatening the hold on economic and political power of the relatively racially privileged.

That the pushback against racially conscious programs like affirmative or positive action has been rationalized in terms of "neutral" principles such as colorblindness and racelessness attests to their transformative possibilities. The reach (back) for "neutrality" seeks to keep existing structural privilege and power in place. Yet the constitutive shortcomings of integrative conditions take for granted the established values and standards by which the racially excluded seeking integration are judged. Integration conventionally conceived thus extends the conditions by which privilege and power are likely to be racially renewed and reinforced, as Justice Harlan famously noted in his colorblinding dissent to *Plessy v. Ferguson* (1896). Introducing the notion of "colorblind," Harlan argued that whites had nothing to fear from opening up competition to all, as their existing skills, training, knowledge, and general superiority would guarantee their continued advancement.

So how does the postracial fit into this historical set of social schemas regarding the racial?

The postracial stands in the experiential legacy articulated here. It is the current extension of experiential nonracialism. Postraciality seeks to avoid completely the questions of structural differentiation. The postracial is the racial condition in denial of the structural. It avoids the fact that the structural forms and fashions the racial, and so too the social advantages, losses, and limits racially ordered. And in these denials and evasions the structural conditions of racial reproduction and racist articulation don't so much lie dormant as persist unattended. For the postracial, race is (to be) racially erased, racisms are thus rendered illegible, disparate impact is reduced to merely unfortunate happenstance. This chapter along with the following two seeks to make evident these broad claims.

Postracial assertion and aspiration

Implicit here is a vacillation between the assertive and aspirational expressions of postracial commitment. It is best captured in the data regarding the racial attitudes of contemporary American "millennial" youth. MTV (2014) commissioned a survey on the racial attitudes of 18 to 24 year olds. The study revealed exactly the tensions at play between the postracial as contemporary claim and future reach, as well as between the individual-experiential and the "dis-appearing" attention to structural conditions historically associated with race.

Significant majorities of the millennials surveyed believe that race is a past problem, that they were brought up to treat everyone equally (84 percent), and that everyone should be treated as equals irrespective of race (91 percent). American millennials, in short – and there is no reason not to believe that comparable rates characterize most other countries too, or at least the trends (Israel may be an obvious exception) – insist they pay no attention to racial differences. They consider themselves to take equality more seriously than their parents do (71 percent). A majority (58 percent) emphasize that racism will wane further as their generation ages and assumes leadership roles in the society.

Over two-thirds claim not to treat those of a different racial background, especially racial minorities, any differently than those of kindred races. And nearly three-quarters insist it would be best never to consider race for any social purpose, while nearly as many argue that doing so forecloses the possibility of the society becoming colorblind. (However, they somewhat inconsistently insist in even larger numbers that celebrating racial differences would better society.) In particular, Barack Obama's election to the US Presidency is taken by a significant majority to show that the opportunities available to racial minorities are equal to those of whites. Effort and smarts are considered to offset whatever lingering disadvantage race still exhibits.

One admires the optimism of youth, even if the underlying data are far more fraught and less encouraging. Digging deeper in the survey responses begins to reveal the racially driven social differentiations at work here. The data illuminate quite sharp if predictable differences between "white" respondents and those of "people of color" (the "racial" designations of the survey) regarding a range of concerns. There are distinct racial differences concerning the first impressions individuals experience and express in interacting with others; in differential teacher treatment by race of students; in racial exclusions at school and the experience of micro-aggressions more generally. There is a roughly twenty-point variance between white and people of color respondents across pretty much all these considerations.

This signals a deeper set of concerns about postracial conditions. Perhaps most revealing is that white respondents nearly twice as readily insisted that racial discrimination against whites is today as pressing a problem as against "racial minorities" (48 to 27 percent). Whites also responded twice as readily as people of color that the government attends too much to the challenges faced by racial minorities (41 to 21 percent). People of color, by contrast, largely considered whites to have more opportunities than racial minorities (65 to 39 percent) (Bouie 2014). These latter responses begin to approach the starker divides between black and white adults in the wake of the Michael Brown shooting in Ferguson in August 2014 and the protests that erupted in its wake. Twice as many black adults as whites polled in a separate Pew (2014) study were concerned that the police response had gone too far (66 to 33 percent), and even more felt that the shooting raised issues of racial concern (80 to 37 percent). Far fewer black respondents than whites, unsurprisingly, thought that they had any confidence in the investigation of the shooting (18 to 52 percent).

These data reveal that attitudes regarding race have grown more complicated. Racial attitudes have always exhibited a degree of contradictoriness, and have often been conflicted. Those in the age of postraciality are made more so not least by their conjoined insistence and denial, their insistence in denial. So much so that this assertive deniability constitutes a central strand in the logic of postraciality, a point on which I will elaborate in the next chapter. Here I want to ask more pointedly: What, buried beneath such data, can one discern under the sign of postraciality about the actual material conditions regarding social positioning in terms of race? And what are the experiences of racist expression, both verbal and physical?

The fact(s) of postraciality

Structurally, almost every index of life conditions, well-being, and social prospects in the United States shows continued significant racial disparity: blacks, Latinos, and Native Americans remain socially worst off on pretty much every index of wellbeing. Of course, countries that elect a mixed-race President or a majority black government demonstrate important advancements over past racial injustices. But, in the case of the United States, the disparities between blacks and Latinos, on one side, and whites, on the other, have mostly been growing, not shrinking as a conventional understanding of postraciality would have it.

Whites, who now comprise a diminishing 64 percent of the US population, own 88 percent of the wealth (in 2010 figures). Blacks, 13 percent of the population, own just 2.7 percent (the ratios are comparable for Latinos/Hispanics). From 1984 to 2009, the real dollar disparity in family wealth between whites and blacks tripled even as the differentiated rate of increase for each narrowed a bit. The family wealth gap of whites compared to blacks and Latinos, respectively, has spiraled to the highest since records were first compiled in 1984. It is now 20:1 (from 12:1) for the former and 18:1 (from 12:1) for the latter. Disaggregated for class, black and brown applicants get denied mortgages for home-ownerships almost 20 percent more often than white applicants. Median wealth of a white family headed by someone with less than a high school diploma today is almost double that of a black family headed by one with a college degree and 20 percent more than that of college-headed Latino families (Kurtzleben 2014).

Consequently, more affluent black and brown residents live in neighborhoods significantly poorer than those of whites with working-class income levels. School segregation by race is the norm, and more likely today than in the late 1960s and 1970s (segregation has increased by 6 percent in the past two decades). Black and Latino students are far more likely to attend more poorly funded schools. When a school increases its student population of color by 10 percent, it experiences an average drop in annual funding of $75 per student. As America grows more diverse (whites will be in the demographic minority by 2043), public schools are becoming more segregated: for the first time in 2014, black, Latino, and Asian students made up a majority of public school attendees. School segregation becomes a perpetual stagnation machine. White schools have no funding incentive to desegregate, and every prompt to absorb and expand segregation.

Black unemployment has remained double the rate of whites' as long as statistics have been kept (the rates are almost identical in France), with the Latino rate falling midway (in 2014, the rates were 12, 6 and almost 9 percent, respectively, with unemployment of

Asians, a supposed "model minority," at just 4 percent). Black job candidates, not unlike potential rental tenants, are routinely discriminated against, often dismissed prior even to an interview once their racial status becomes evident. White men and women earn higher weekly wages than black men and women, who in turn earn more than Latinos (the differences are between $30 and $50 per week per category). Skilled job categories remain dominated by white workers. The "33 whitest jobs in America" range from veterinarians, farmers, mining machinists, speech pathologists, electricians, and sheet metal workers to speech pathologists, airplane pilots, construction supervisors and managers, as well as architects, CEOs, and environmental scientists. Whites occupy more than 90 percent of positions in each of these job categories, despite constituting less than 70 percent of the overall population (Thompson 2013).

Black and brown people are far more likely than comparably classed whites to be stopped and searched for no reason other than their visible racial profile. In 2011, nearly 700,000 people were stopped and searched on the street (more than one every minute), over 90 percent of them black and brown. While the numbers dropped fourfold in 2012, a person was still stopped every five minutes or less. A little over 10 percent were arrested as a result, overwhelmingly for marijuana possession. Despite then Mayor Bloomberg's rationalization of the policy that blacks and Latinos represented a larger proportion of violent criminals, almost no arrests were made for weapons possession, and very few for violent crimes. Black and brown men, especially, are more likely to be violently treated by the police, and consequently to be arrested and ultimately imprisoned largely for non-violent drug offenses. ("Stop and frisk" was ruled unconstitutional in 2013.)

Nationwide, African Americans suffer violence at the hands of police across the United States at almost twice the rate of Latinos and nearly four times the rate of whites (4.4, 2.3, and 1.2 percent, respectively) (Brooks 2014; cf. Lee 2014). Those recklessly killed by police across American cities have almost invariably been black, as the recent killings of Michael Brown, Eric Garner, Tamir Rice, and others have so chillingly evidenced. In 2012, one study shows, a black man in the United States was killed by police, security guards, or vigilantes every twenty-eight hours (Hudson 2013). According to FBI data, between 2007 and 2014, police killed 400 people per annum, a quarter of them black. Though making up approximately 26 percent of the US population, blacks and Latinos are made to serve up something like 62 percent of the US prison population.

Nearly one third of black men between the ages of 20 and 29 are currently under some form of criminal justice supervision (prison/jail, parole, probation), and have an approximately 30 percent chance of spending time in prison across their lives. It is revealing that, today, more black men in the United States reside in prison than attend college. The impacts are cross-generational, with massive multiplier effects: a little more than 4 percent of American children have a parent in prison; for African-American kids, it is over 10 percent.

These characterizations begin to blur the lines between the structural and the experiential. They indicate the ways structural social positioning heightens the likelihood of racist experience. Such racial experience, in turn, often reinforces the structures, keeping them in place. African-American life expectancy remains upwards of four years shorter than that of white Americans due in large part to higher diabetes, cancer, stress, murder, and stroke rates. The contrast in South Africa is even starker: white life expectancy is over 60, that of blacks under 50. In Israel life expectancy of Jews is around 82; for Palestinians in the West Bank it is approximately 72 (and at least a year less in Gaza). These life expectancy differentials bear out Ruth Wilson Gilmore's (2007) conception of racism as producing premature death.

Two broader claims are in order here. First, these differential conditions are taken to be a function of individual self-responsibility, or its lack. US Congressman Steve King insisted that Eric Garner's death by police strangulation was caused by his own obesity and asthma, thus reducing the structural to the experiential and individualized agency. Second, such structural conditions make all experience in societies marked by comparable conditions more or less racial. Far from being beyond race, the postracial has made race almost unrecognizably part of the "natural" fabric of the social and the social fabric of the natural order of things. Call this the anthropocenic racial, the "anthroporacial." I will elaborate the logic by which this perverse turn has been realized in the following chapter.

The proliferating experiences of racial humiliation, dismissal, and aggression begin to render such a bald and bold claim more plausible. One can find almost daily accounts of racist micro-aggressions, racial humiliations, condescending dismissals and blatant insensitivities (Rankine 2014). Some may seem inconsequential, even trivial, not least when viewed in isolation. But many are not, and even those that appear immaterial when viewed alone become more consequential when linked as part of a larger culture and daily experience. Often when digging deeper into the seemingly isolated and dismissable events one can find deeper connections to more obviously troubling structural arrangements. Racist trivia rarely express themselves unrelated to these larger structures of sustained racisms, extending them in turn.

From the 2008 US Presidential race onwards, it has largely been assumed that a vote against Obama is simply an expressed disagreement with his policies. That would be fair enough. But there has been widespread racially charged sentiment, prompted and reproduced by opposition politicians and their supporters. Kentucky voters in 2008 declared they would gladly vote for a Democrat were it not for their staunch opposition to electing an African-American President. Effectively they were acting on the commitment that the US President presumptively must be white. Indeed, by voting to support an Obama policy such as "Obamacare" (the Affordable Care Act), a politician has been considered not just to vote for the black President but effectively to be "tarred" with the brush of blackness, and so to be similarly unsupportable.

Michael Tesler and David Sears (2010) have found that in the United States today race not only marks the divide in political views. Whites' attitudes towards black people now drive broader attitudes about policies hitherto long uncorrelated with – and so not evidently related to – race. Attitudes about health care provision are the obvious but far from the only case. People's beliefs about whether the unemployment rate or the size of government, tax rates, and the numbers who are being served by the state are increasing or decreasing are now more often driven by their racial attitudes than by the data (Chait 2014). Similarly, views about the United States growing "too (racially) diverse" impact political responses to immigration and "securing the border" even against entry by children seeking family reunification or refuge from intense violence in their home countries. Racial consideration, if not calculation, impacts voting rights also. Across the United States, concerns to extend white political control have prompted legislative support requiring state-issued voter identification to delimit (non-existent) voter fraud by poorer voters of color. The implicit aim is to delimit electoral advantage by discouraging voting by people of color, who tend largely to support the Democrats (Ginsburg 2014).

White reviewers consistently rate identical legal briefs significantly lower, finding more error in them when told the author was black rather than white. Mistakes by authors considered black were immediately attributed to incompetence; identical errors by those presumed white were deemed the product of inexperience

(Your Black World 2014). This is consistent with a broader finding that white faculty at universities tend overwhelmingly to respond to emails and queries from white male students rather than from students of color or women. Recent studies have found that the more white Americans psychologically associate especially violent crime with blacks, the less likely they are to support reform of racially charged criminal statutes such as "stop and frisk" or three-strikes reforms they might otherwise be disposed to embrace. All this clearly disadvantages people of color (and women) in grading, hiring, employment advancement, and criminal justice. It thus links the experiential to the structural in ways more causal than correlational.

These "born-again" racial sensibilities and racist dispositions are far from limited to the "postracial" United States. The Swedish government announced in August 2014 that all references to race in Swedish legislation will be erased. While rationalized in the name of delegitimizing "the social construct of race," this evasive erasure of race from legislation would seem to hamper, if not rule out, the enactment of laws specifically targeting racially driven animus in public life. For example, throughout Europe, black and brown football players have been vilified on the field, taunted as monkeys, and pelted with bananas. Black cabinet ministers in France and Italy, in both cases the first black women to hold cabinet positions in their countries, have been repeatedly disparaged and demeaned in exactly these terms. A laser image of President Obama with a banana stuffed in his mouth was projected onto the outer wall of the former US embassy in Moscow. Other "monkey-fied" images of Obama have circulated widely in Russia, where black residents have often faced violent beatings by racist Russian youth (Mazza 2014). US-generated websites, many associated with Tea Party groups, have posted thousands of demeaning caricatures of the President and his family represented as monkeys and baboons, with the view to dehumanizing the man, delegitimating his Presidency, weakening his social standing, and undermining policies he has sought to enact.

Animalizing postraciality

Monkeys, baboons, orangutans, and mules have been central media of racially characterized dehumanization, the projection of degraded intelligence and delimited rational capacity. Animalization and bestialization have long been integral to the history of racist representation, perhaps even more so than the objectification or "thingification" of people. Things may be easily usable and discardable. But they tend to be passive until put to use. The reification of people into the condition of "thinghood" renders them objects of pure control rather than the interlocutors of (sometimes contentious) relation. The thingification of humanity is rarely ever complete, the reductive drive to thinghood bound to disappoint the racist committed to complete exploitative control. Animalization offers another mode available to racial power.

Like things, animals can be put to use, rendered pliable. They can be made sport, purveyors of derisive pleasure, rounded up or herded to instrumental purpose. But in being put to work, teased, prodded, and kicked, they can push back and give grief. US Congressman Steve King again provides an example here, with his collapse of animalization and objectification in characterizing undocumented Mexican migrants as mostly drug "mules" with "calves the size of cantaloupes" from carrying "75 lb sacks of marijiuana" across the desert border. He was confronted at a political campaign fundraiser by two young undocumented Chicano/a "Dreamers" (Immoral Minority 2014). Both patriotic college graduates (one a lawyer), they had been brought as young children to the United States by their parents. In an embarrassing video that went viral, King is caught in the exchange both defending and refusing to acknowledge his racist comments.

Lest one think this an anomalous expression by a politician under unexpected pressure, not a week later Rep. King would reiterate his barely latent racism. The Congressional Black Caucus had called for a thorough investigation of possible racial profiling by the Ferguson police force in the wake of Michael Brown's killing by a local police officer and the subsequent militarized policing response. In a radio interview with a conservative talk show, King could not restrain himself from uttering almost incomprehensibly that:

> The idea of no racial profiling ... I've seen the video. It looks to me like you don't need to bother with that particular factor because they all appear to be of a single origin, I should say, a continental origin might be the way to phrase that .... (Fang 2014)

For King, there was no racial profiling by the police officer who killed Brown and underlying the resulting police response to the protests because everyone in Ferguson (but for the police, as it turns out) is of "continental origin." Unable to bring himself to blurt out that all black people originated in "Africa," King reveals a stunning lack of historical knowledge about the "one drop" processes by which black Americans became African American. No matter, he denies any racial profiling at play here because in Ferguson the police had only blacks to pick on. Racial profiling, however, does not just mean that black folk are targeted. It means exactly that they are the *only* ones picked on, and for no reasonable purpose other than suspecting that they must be up to no good *because* they are black. That the population of the small city of Ferguson is a little more than 60 percent African American in any case makes a mockery of King's folly. He exemplifies the now common critical observation that if one is racist regarding one racially defined group, one is likely to be so against most all others not one's own. King's implausible deniability is little more than the classic denial of (racist) implausibility.

Racist projections, like King's, in turn have served to (re)produce and rationalize limitations on access, the curtailment of educational opportunities, and processes of deskilling and occupational restriction, extraction and exploitation. Animals, and human animals, can be enticed, entrapped, or physically elicited through beatings to produce more, always more. But failing that, they may still act out, become liabilities or threats, assume or be presumed to embody bestial characteristics by pushing back or stubbornly refusing. After living out their value-adding usefulness or threatening social homogeneity, coherence, and stability, the (post)racially animalized can be guiltlessly culled and curtailed, killed off, eliminated.

The sustained street protests by local town residents that followed Michael Brown's police shooting in Ferguson, not unlike those that followed the Mark Duggan killing in London in 2012, were met by a massively militarized police response that embarrassed even military representatives owing to its excess and ineptitude. Protestors were confronted with riot gear, heavy weaponry and armored vehicles, tear gas and rubber bullets. National journalists and local politicians alike found themselves under arrest pretty much for just showing up. (It was reported by Anonymous [2014], the hacktivist network, that the St Louis County police chief who was leading this massively militarized police response had spent a month in 2011 being trained by the Israeli Defense Force in counter-insurgency strategy, at the expense of the American Anti-Defamation League, the vocal pro-Israeli lobby group in the United States.) One of the white St Louis County police officers dispatched to Ferguson in full military riot gear "to keep the peace" was videotaped shouting at the largely African-American protestors, "Bring it all, you fucking animals. Bring it."

Todat these explicit expressions of animalization and their heightened denials most readily come from the lips of Israelis, notably but far from only in the case of Palestine and especially Gaza. Ehud Barak, former Israeli Prime Minister and Defense Minister, once characterized Israel as "a villa in the jungle." *Latma TV*, a popular satirical Israeli television program, aimed at skewering intellectual leftists, has represented Africans as banana-eating baboons. Such characterizations, in turn, came to be directed by some Israelis, especially on the right, at recently arrived East African refugees.

In July 2014 three Israel teenage boys were kidnapped and killed while hitchhiking home after attending yeshiva school in the West Bank. That they were sent to a yeshiva school in the West Bank and in no way discouraged from hitchhiking in what is effectively hostile occupied territory speaks to Israeli presumptions of ownership and possession. After all, three West Bank Palestinian teenagers could hardly go to school in Israel, and if they so much as attempted to hitchhike they would be immediately picked up – by the Israeli police. The boys' disappearance, blamed questionably on Hamas operatives, became the initial pretext for Israel's 2014 pervasive bombing, re-invasion, and re-occupation of Gaza. Prime Minister Benjamin Netanyahu immediately called the kidnappers "human animals."

The Israeli rhetorical barrage against Gazans in particular, Palestinians more generally, was quickly heightened by lowering Palestinian status to the level of animals on the ground and underground. Israelis overwhelmingly refer to Palestinians as "Arabs," at once identifying Palestinians with generalized Arab hostility to them in the region while alienating Palestinian presence from Israel/Palestine by nominating them out of existence. This sense of elimination by renomination, a common state strategy in relation to rewriting the map of Israel's landscape, is reinforced by referring to Gaza as the "Casbah." This is a characterization readily circulating in the military as a result of widespread training use of Pontecorvo's film *The Battle of Algiers*.

Palestinians have been increasingly animated as "snakes in tunnels" squirming their way into Israel to carry out terroristic plots, or as insects crawling across the landscape. They are deemed maggots, cockroaches, and vermin out to infect Israel's body politic, a decaying rot eating at the nation's democratic social fabric. Moshe Feiglin, deputy Speaker of the Israeli Knesset, urged the state to "concentrate" the "snakes" in Gaza in order to "exterminate" the threat. Another Knesset member, Ayelet Shaked, approvingly shared on her Facebook page an article by a conservative Israeli journalist calling for the death of the mothers of Palestinian children characterized as "little snakes." Her post attracted thousands of Facebook "likes." Animalization is a tactical necropolitics, delivering elimination if not complete extermination.

In South Africa, elevated as a crucial experiment regarding a smooth transition to postracial democracy, a photograph of a grinning young Afrikaner in military fatigue bush shirt was posted to a Facebook page in 2011. He was brandishing a rifle while kneeling over an apparently dead body of a young black boy as if over the carcass of his slaughtered beastly prey. Captioned (in Afrikaans), "I don't like a fool, so what?," the Facebook page quickly generated over 600 "friends." The Afrikaner, going by the name of "Terrorblanche" (a salute to Eugene Terreblanche, the South African white supremacist separatist), explained that he had paid the young boy to pose for the picture (James 2011; Swart 2011).

More pliable than thinghood, animalization has long combined the exploitative and exterminationist models and mandates of the racial. What perhaps is new about the postracial – or really renewed, in novel ways ramified and elasticized – is that the exterminating mandate of raciality has not simply been resurrected. It simultaneously dissolves the stain of the racial, rendering it largely invisible, erasing the referential chains linking exterminating missions to any signs of explicit raciality. In the face of that invisibilizing erasure, if one attempts to make those links one is deemed hallucinatory in the rhetoric of the mainstream media. One is literally seeing or imagining the non-existent, the unimaginable. Post-raciality is nothing less than mystification.

Racial thingification – reducing those identified racially to things – instrumentalizes and rationalizes the exploitative and extractive. Animalization, by contrast, tends to instrumentalize and rationalize the exterminating mandate in the name of killing off the threat. Domestication renders the animal non-threatening. It anthropomorphizes the animal, humanizing it precisely. Hence raciality's recourse always to the most demeaned and degraded, the most threatening animalizations. The reference is to animals considered unclean, bearing disease, the source of viral outbreaks. Perversely, the postracial heightens the likelihood of the recourse to these degradations precisely by looking to expunge the racially explicit from them, by refusing to acknowledge their racist articulation. And in the refusal it acknowledges the unacceptability of racist expression while denying the implication. Degrading animalization, it could be said, is the preferred expression of postraciality.

Postraciality, like racial modalities almost always, offers itself as an immunization against the viral and pathogenic threats of mixture. It serves as a bulwark against the uncertainties and unsettlements of heterogeneous and diverse socialities not only external to the nation but more or less invisible in its midst. Like all racialities, the postracial seeks to establish a single standard, an absolute paradigm of singular value predicated on the commands historically identified with the power of the racially dominant. The postracial is an immunology, a prophylactic, against racial distinction and differentiation, as much against a race-criticality as against racial injustice. It provides immunity to the sacred community, protecting its sovereignty from the polluting threats of the non-belonging, locally and globally (Esposito 2008).

So, postraciality is less a credible factual claim about contemporary conditions than a projection of their futurity. The "post" here is what the future as a matter of fact and norm should amount to and look like. Postraciality undertakes to advance (oftentimes an even more extreme version of) contemporary racist conditions as tomorrow's present – and to do so in the name of a sterilizing erasure of once explicit racist expression. It is in the refusal that the expression is explicitly racist. This refusal is racist both in intention and in effect. In the latter case, as with sexual violence, it makes the wrongdoing the target's fault, something she brings upon herself. The new future normal is the projection of an ever-present. Apocalypse now.

On neoliberalizing presumptions, structural racism is no longer a matter of concern. It follows that post-raciality is the deletion of explicitly racial policy. Racisms are reducible to individualized expression, the anomaly of the occasional outburst. Government regulation of expressive sociality is anathema. So, there is neither need nor place for regulating policy on race. Consider US Supreme Court Chief Justice John Roberts's now widely repeated (apparent) tautology that to stop discrimination on the basis of race we have to stop discriminating on the basis of race. As neoliberalization would have it, ending such discrimination is a matter not of government regulation requiring its cessation. It is a matter rather of individuals no longer finding they need to express themselves in these ways, though they are free to do so, absent government involvement, should they so prefer. The cost of continuing racist expression, if any, is to the bottom line of the person expressing him- or herself in racist terms.

This turns racism simply into a calculation, an economic calculus. And, of course, if a person's or organization's racist expression promotes profitability – bringing fans to the race track or football stadium, promoting the sale of racist paraphernalia such as t-shirts, music, and magazines off white power websites, attracting viral notoriety, popularity, and so on – there is nothing standing in its way. Nothing, that is, other than individual disapprobation or counter-action like a boycott to put an end to it.

Postraciality, far from ending racial discrimination, is its dis-appearance. Like prostitution swept from city street corners, it simply gravitates elsewhere in the social landscape. I turn in the chapter that follows to mapping out in detail the logics of this new landscape of post-raciality, of the anthroporacial.

THREE

Postracial logics

Postraciality is the aspirational, if not yet fully realized, mode in terms of which contemporary racisms are projected. Conceptually, postraciality owes its emergence to post-World War II skepticism about biologizing racial claims. This skepticism heightened the gathering concerns around centuries of racial naturalism, beginning concretely to institutionalize the drive to racelessness. In the early 1950s, the various UN Statements on Race sought first to undermine all use of race to classify humans and then, in the wake of the ensuing pushback, to invoke the term only in broad descriptive use to refer to perceivable physical distinction.

This emergent skepticism regarding racial distinction was further cemented by three developments: the civil rights movement's insistence on "colorblindness"; the explicit commitment of the prevailing anti-apartheid coalition in South Africa to a notion of "nonracialism," expressed most forcefully in the Freedom Charter; and continental European insistence that "race" only be used to refer to animal sub-species. The idea here was to resist any social, political, or legal use of race for discriminatory purpose, to elevate or privilege members of one group at the expense of others. In short, notions like "colorblindness" and "nonracialism" became compelling in the cauldron of political movements, struggles, and campaigns.

These entangled threads of commitment to racelessness were at once descriptive and prescriptive. They were further knotted together by the forces of globalization. Globalization forged the intensifyingly interactive connectivity of everywhere, everyone, and most everything. If Galileo's dictum that "all is in motion" expressed modernity's driving ontology, the motto for late modern globalization is that "all is connected." In this hotpot, peoples and cultures supposedly grew less opaque, more familiar, less foreign to each other. Cultural expression quickly became embodied in commodification and the romance with consumption goods.

Against this backdrop of globalizing mixture, postracial racelessness assumed the contemporary default regarding racial conditions. Behind the supposed erasure of government-sanctioned racial classification and privilege, racial reference, accusation, and restriction proliferated. These tensions played out politically in a tug-of-war between the forces of colorblindness and multiculturalism referenced earlier. Racelessness emerged in this struggle as the principal articulation of postraciality.

Racelessness and postraciality

Colorblindness and nonracialism manifested as terms of commitment in the deeply political texture of struggle in the 1950s. Yet, despite (and in part exactly because of) their elaboration in response to racially fraught politics, colorblindness and nonracialism became quiescent, detached. They came to evade the fraught conditions at issue. Race is taken actively to divide. Conventional nonracial and colorblind dispositions assumed over time the conceptual impetus to ignore. The initial sense of belligerent refusal underwriting the struggles gave way to passivity. This passivity reflects no longer having to grapple with the troubling concerns of a perceived past far from passed.

Postraciality has become most deeply marked by this passive detachment. The "postracial" is in denial of its political thrust. It is not just born out of globalizing movements. It transfigures raciality conceptually, culturally, and politically. In neoliberal spirit, the postracial individualizes responsibility. It renders individuals solely accountable for their own actions and expressions, not for their group's. Similarly, it refuses to ascribe responsibility to one's purported racial group for the actions and expressions of the group's individual members. Here, neoliberal skepticism about the agency of social groups generally has encouraged the erosion of racial connectivity, and by extension any ontological claim to racial groups more broadly.

Liberalism's economic anthropology is centered on *homo oeconomicus*. "Economic Man" supposedly chooses and acts rationally to maximize individual self-interest, whether in consumption or interpersonal relations. By extension, neoliberal anthropology, as Foucault (2008: 147–8) suggests, rests squarely on the heroic "Man of Enterprise." Enterprising Man is one who competes and produces, invents and creates things. But *he* is also making things up, the man adept at managing and manipulating mixtures, social intercourse, and mash-ups. Committed to innovation and design, he works at prising open entry for the sake ultimately of nothing but self-advantage, self-possibility, self-profit. If there is social benefit as a result, it would be a fortuitous value added. Yet that cannot be the goal or mandate. Enterprising Man makes things on the basis of innovative design, making things happen by inventiveness and self-invention. Fabrication and self-making, creation and re-creation serve as the presiding sensibilities of the time. Looking good and acting awesome, he is self-minded in flaunting prowess and profit. But he also projects braggadocio and whatever he can get away with. Seemingly in full control even in bordering on being out of control, he networks only with the like-minded and like-looking. He is *Mad Men* embodied, *American Psycho* realized (for a telling illustration, cf. Morse 2014).

These sensibilities make evident too why recreational activities – extreme sports and extensive game playing especially – have been transformed, literally re-created, from what we do occasionally, a hobby, to a prevailing mode of profitable capitalization and professionalizing practice. Nor should the driving racialities of these most popular representations be lost on us.

In keeping with the neoliberalizing thrusts of individualization, self-making, and the proliferation of enterprise, the postracial condition doubles racial response. Responsibility for racist expression is reduced to an individualized account, to a bad apple, a rogue element. This denies responsibility to structural conditions or larger social forces. For neoliberalizing postraciality, racism is an anomaly, the mark of a past historical moment. It is an irritating residue to be gotten over as quickly as possible, or even simply recreational ("I was just kidding"). (For explicit examples of the latter in the

British context, including legal implications, cf. Sambrook 2014.) Racism remains merely a stain on the social fabric, to be washed away as quickly as possible.

Self-production here applies as much to the making of racial identity and self-expression as it does to any other mode of expression or product(ion). So one is licensed to make up one's personal racial life story and social identity for the sake of self-advantage. Virtual possibilities – for example, identities – obviously expand and elasticize the reach while multiplying the range of this self-making. In doing so, individualized responsibility is instantaneously magnified while its importance, its seriousness, is discounted, especially in moments when one might be called to defend one's choices, projections, and fabrications. Social life takes on a game-like quality, with all the implications this might entail.

Racelessness today has become something of a cult(ure). It is evidenced by the fact that the driving tendency regarding discussions of race has become taking seriously, and literally, the question whether "we" – in this or that society – have reached the state of the postracial yet. The prevailing response among progressives and conservatives alike, if for contrasting reasons, is that obviously we have not. Progressives point as evidence to the slew of contemporary data of the kind offered in Chapter 2 concerning extensive structural inequities, as well as the stream of often violent racisms to which black and brown people are daily subjected.

Conservatives, almost exclusively white, point to what they believe has been a surge of anti-white racism, even while insisting that anti-black racism has receded (David 2014). They find evidence of this supposed anti-white racism especially in the persistence and proliferation of preferential treatment programs for blacks at the expense of whites; in the escalating, purportedly bogus charges of racism against whites; and in the silencing of white self-defense (Auster 2008). One widely circulating internet image reveals a young white man holding a placard reading, "It doesn't matter what this sign says, you'll call it racism anyway." Such projections are strikingly similar among conservatives and some (lapsed) liberals in the United States and South Africa, in Britain and Europe, Australia, and Canada. But they are reflected also in what Telles (2014) characterizes as the "pigmentocracies" of Brazil and Latin America more broadly. In societies marked by heterogeneous color terms for racial coding, such as Brazil, racial discrimination is both increasingly recognized today and broadly denied by the elites, who tend overwhelmingly to be white (Araújo 2014).

There is something obvious, even predictable, about these responses. The obviousness is reflected in the contemporary hyper-racial world. Barely a day goes by without a racially charged incident or expression surfacing. And the predictability is driven by the expectation that those on the left and right would respond to the question of postraciality exactly as they do. All of this, however, gives in to the question regarding the reality of postraciality: it assumes a literal understanding of the term; it presupposes its credibility, presumes its seriousness, perhaps even its coherence; and it prompts a public performativity, on both sides of the divide. It takes for granted a conception and comprehension of "the postracial condition" widely ascribed to, about which there has been all too little critical public discussion.

Racelessness, at least in a racially ordered social landscape, ironically is never raceless. Against the thick background histories of racisms, racelessness expresses racial discrimination through other means. So, racelessness is not the commitment to ending injustices associated with racial designation, to ending racisms. Rather, it is the insistence on racial erasure, thus rendering racially inspired or inflected injustices more difficult, even impossible, to discern. It implicitly extends racial injustice by leaving it (largely) unidentified, untouched, untouchable, because lacking the terms by which actually to identify the expression as such.

Racisms (re)produce the non-belonging and the differentiated. They define and identify the unwanted, the pathological, the unsettled. And they refine and (re) place the unsettling and the threatening, both within and external to the social boundaries at stake. Racisms in fact trade on transforming the subjects of imagined threats and concerns into real ones. Racial targeting to marginalize – to exploit, expropriate, eliminate or erase, dismiss or diminish – is far from antique or some lingering remnant of uncivilized pasts. Racisms remain embedded in the maintenance of social order by means of their immunological dictates and measures. Made by the modern, racisms are key technologies of constituting and governing populations today.

The question to face here, then, is not whether we have reached the aspirational state of the postracial seemingly promised by Obama's election in the United States and the ending of formalized apartheid with Mandela's election in South Africa. Perhaps it was naïve to think that five hundred years of cemented racisms could be dismantled in the wink of an election or two. It seems more revealing to ask now what work – what racial work, exactly – the "postracial" is doing, as conception and claim. What is the recourse to postraciality producing by design or implication, as social conception and ordering, as racial articulation?

The racial work of postraciality

To begin responding to these questions, then: postraciality is committed to erasing any racial categorization or naming by *public* institutions, while protecting *private* racial arrangements and expression. Racial distinction, derogation, and displacement are registered in the name of the no longer nameable, in denial of intention, disclaiming causation, or even explicit expression (Gunaratnam and Murji 2013). The public recession of race has given way to its private inflation. Deflation of its *formal* governing power is more than offset by the investment in the political currency of nationalism liberated by deregulating racial privatization.

The presumption that race is no longer socially relevant plays out variously, coagulating in conditions whose unnameability renders them increasingly unspecifiable. These conditions tend to disadvantage those socially characterized as not white. The insistence that states (should) no longer engage in racially discriminatory laws, structures, and practices regarding the people they govern and impact has multiple implications. It exonerates states of any racial commitment. It silences explicit racial and racist expression, pushing them underground. But more deeply, it shields states from charges that their conduct discriminates racially.

Counterfactually, this shielding makes it more rather than less likely that states assertively engage in practices and extend structures they once would have had no hesitation in identifying racially, as racist. Postracially committed states now fail even to recognize them. So this purging of racial characterization by the state actually heightens the possibility of racially impacting state violence, either unrecognized as such or, more likely, stripped of the inhibiting charges that its practices or structures are racist. Israel's treatment of Palestinians, especially Gazans, exemplifies the point. Israelis increasingly express degrading judgments about Palestinians and the state readily engages in deadly actions against them that once would have been condemned as racist. The disappearance of racial characterization sometimes leads to heightening racist violence, even dramatically, rather than ending or diminishing it (as in the increased Islamophobia and anti-Semitism following France's banning of the use of "race" or "ethnicity" in legislation).

The postracial era we are now taken collectively to inhabit is shorthand for the state of generalized social equality of opportunity, enterprise, and competitiveness supposedly marking contemporary social arrangements. Equal opportunity is the characterization of conditions from which overt impediments to entry and competition have nominally been removed. Far from equality of outcomes, no longer is the driving criterion for equality of opportunity the preparedness to compete – for places at university, or employment, or the means to start a business, an enterprise. Rather, it is the minimal barrier to apply, to be considered, to have parents with sufficient means to help out. That anyone can apply, no matter what their racial characterization, level of preparedness, professional qualifications, or familial means, suffices to meet the bar of postracial equality.

This is a long drop off from the standard liberal commitment to equality of opportunity taken as sharing a baseline level of preparedness, possibility, and access. Any commitment expressed to a more robust equity in outcome or distribution is now quickly dismissed as socialist. This way of expressing the commitment has become especially explicit in the United States, as Supreme Court Justice Ruth Bader Ginsburg (2014) recently bemoaned. But as a central entailment of neoliberal presumption it likely holds far more broadly, if less explicitly, even in states with more robust

71

egalitarian histories. As Foucault (2008) puts it regarding neoliberality, this represents a new mode of social and economic regulation.

Thin equality of opportunity embeds another, less predicted mode of social regulation and effect. The removal of formal racial barriers to competition and enterprise has licensed erosion of barriers to free *racial* expression. Individuals have felt free, even entitled (Essed 2013), to say almost anything crossing their minds about those regarded as racially different from them. Whites especially have reiterated and reinforced the most pernicious stereotypes. Living in a postracial state seems to have entailed the possibility of subjects expressing themselves in ways as blatantly and explicitly racist as they choose with little risk of being called on it. When occasionally called to task, they readily swat away the charge as unintended, misperceived, simply silly, or an uncontestable truth of personal experience.

Examples abound. Before he was murdered on a busy East Amsterdam street, filmmaker Theo van Gogh readily referred to Muslims, without raising a Dutch eyebrow, as "goat-fuckers." On the Fox News discussion forum *The Five*, co-host Anna Tantaros, using Muslims, Islam, and ISIS interchangeably, insisted that "They [Muslims] have been [beheading] for hundreds and hundreds of years if you study the history of Islam. This isn't a surprise. You can't solve it with dialogue. You can't solve it with a summit. You solve it with a bullet to the head. It's the only thing these people understand" (Cheung 2014). Postracial racist expression ranges from the frivolous to the extreme, with potentially deadly implications.

Those expressing themselves in racist ways now increasingly do not apologize for the expression or the harm incurred, nor even for the offense. They apologize rather as *if* offense has been taken by the targeted. In that conditionality the racism itself becomes hypothetical, vanishing as not really real. Any intentionality is denied, as if racism were only possible by premeditation. And then the denial of any racism, intended or otherwise, is denied, erasing in that denial of denial any traces of (possible) occurrence.

A recent instance, one among many, involves a local city councilman in a small Missouri town apologizing for posting to his Facebook page blatantly racist images of Obama. When criticized, he declared himself "a very active Republican." Opposed to Obama's policies, as any Republican would be, he was merely having fun at the President's expense, expecting no harm to come of it. He declaratively intended no racist harm (Garcia 2014). No intention, no willfulness, so no racism? In his not meaning to express racist harm, he seeks to remove any trace of racist meaning or harm from his expression. As if erasure were so simple, the easiness of the gesture making the offending images even more publicly available, continuing to circulate in their deniability.

A Tea Party group in Kansas, the Patriot Freedom Alliance, depicted President Obama on its website in the animalizing figure of a skunk. The accompanying text insisted that "Skunks are half black, half white, and almost everything it [*sic*] does stinks." In the face of criticism, a group spokesman simply denied the claim to be racist (notwithstanding the longstanding racist identification of black people not only as animals but also as stinking). No explanation is needed because, divorced from any racial legacy in which it stands, the charge of racism makes no sense. The nominalism of just calling a skunk a skunk is divided by the firewall of denial from calling a monkey a monkey, or a "nigger" a "nigger."

The postracial is not just the denial of lingering racial conditionality, its discarding of the racial to the past. It is, as I suggested above, more than that: the "post" in the "postracial" is the denial also about postracial *denial*, deniability's recursive refusal. I assert my (non)racial, my postracial innocence not just by denying that I any longer, or ever, make (or made) racial reference or

mobilized racist exclusion; I now further deny that I am
in denial. I can't possibly be racist now because I never
was then. My tolerance now – my openness to all otherness, or even more strongly to all *my* otherness – is
evidence of my characteristic tolerance. So I couldn't
have been racist then too. I can't be in denial because
– tolerant then, as now – denial was never an issue.
Thus postraciality reaches also for the denial of denial.
I have turned my historical past into an empty white
canvas, perhaps even a canvas of whiteness – or better
yet a canvassing of whiteness. The postracial is nothing
less than the vanishing point of race, and the supposedly fading pinprick of racism.

In the name of postraciality, political and demographic exclusions become erased from consciousness
and consideration. As Saree Makdisi (2010: 554–5)
puts it in the case of excising Palestinians from Israel
and to increasing degrees from Palestine more broadly,
they become so "clean, pure and total" as to cease being
"recognizable" as such at all. This induces the erasure of
erasure itself, leaving in place consideration only of
those who define and determine the terms of consideration to begin with.

By the same account, postraciality enables not just
the denial that one is engaged in racism. It renders
opaque and invisible the terms by which the charge of

racism against its historical agents or their inheritors is realizable. The denial of racism's denial runs so deep it no longer needs to be said. The founding pillar on which postraciality has been built now makes invisible the (racial) terms and conditions on which racisms historically have been predicated. Ironically, and not inconsequentially, it potentially leaves unanchored and meaningless the very significance of the term "postraciality" itself.

Postraciality, accordingly, remains enigmatically a raciality. It is a raciality that in its enigmatic drive to exceed the bounds and bonds of race, to multiply or proliferate the inputs in capital's ever-expansive quest for profit and power, does so by resorting to denial. This denial is not just of historical conditions but of the contemporary constraints – the legacy of racially driven inequalities – structured by those historical conditions reproduced across time. The postracial denies the historical conditions and their legacy effects. It buries, alive, those very conditions that are the grounds of its own making. Buried alive, those conditions continue to constitute a hold, a handicap, a disability at the intersection of race and class on those still forced to bear their load. Class standing mitigates and mediates the load, to be sure. It admits some into a register of the privileges and relative power of whiteness, without dissolving or compensating (completely) for the accumulated disadvantages.

It follows that the postracial empties out the racial, conventionally conceived, of its "classic" meanings. It thus opens the racial (in its empty silences) to be filled with any meanings chosen, at hand, fabricated, made up. This "filling" becomes a "fulfilling" – a prophecy, prediction, what is divined, always already known – of history, personality, productivity, national character, national or group (ethnic, racial) "personality": They are not ready to live among us, for advancement, for democracy. They are lazy, criminals, won't work. They are dirty, uncouth, disease-bearing. They reject "Anglo-American law" and the neutralizing justice for which it is taken to stand, as the Lt Governor of Missouri put it in dismissing the protests by black residents of Ferguson after the killing of Michael Brown. The postracial, in short, reinscribes destiny in the name of its supposed denial.

Postraciality, accordingly, is pure political theology. Political theology does not just pose in secular terms the central theological commitments of a tradition but projects its modes of thinking, frames of analysis, and prevailing social relations. It embeds political rationality within aspirations of transcendentalism, political power in ultimately unchallengeable claims to sovereignty, political membership in the structures of state sacralization. Political theology manifests as it transcendentally (re)inscribes unchallengeable, because sanctified, *conviction*.

What is turned into the racially silent, the silently racial – its ghostly presence burying alive racial histories – becomes the perfect medium for what I call "make believe." "Make believe" compels belief in the unbelievable, the unseen "truth" inscribed yet again in socialities of the skin. These socialities are presumed without naming (because they no longer have to be named). They are evidenced experientially (as communities of experience) while lacking independent warrant. Political conviction denuded of its explicit politics becomes the given, the taken-for-granted of skin-deep sociality, the political Truth of our time.

These commitments can now be asserted shamelessly because they don't have to account for the apparent cover of classic racial terms. Absent racial terms, intentionality no longer has to be denied. It simply can be said never to have crossed my mind. Transcendental conviction substitutes for political or practical reason (in the Aristotelian sense), producing a politics of make believe, of compulsion, but now no longer nameable because it lacks any terms of reference. Enterprising and inventive make believe becomes as much the raison d'être of social representation and rationalization as of economic expression and competition. "I felt my life threatened by this black man. They are always armed and aggressive. So I had no option but to shoot him dead."

Postraciality proceeds, then, by way of *deflection* (from attending to racial disparity). In more intimate settings I am simply co-existing with those like me, in looks and likes, vision and viewpoints, means and manageability. This deflection enables the assertion of the racial in its social conditions and conditionality without calling attention to the raciality of its condition. Israel in Palestine offers the exemplary case in point. But then so do suburban whites in the St Louis suburbs who readily dismiss the protestors on the streets of Ferguson a few miles away as "doing what they want to do," as "just taking the opportunity to satisfy their desire for junk," and as "a lot of outside people coming in" to make trouble (Ioffe 2014).

So, racism expresses itself in the extreme because it is delinked from the constraints of its being named as racial injustice. The avoidances of racial reference, of being named in and on these terms – being named as a pariah condition – evidence the lengths to which privileged folks, folks asserting privilege while claiming disprivilege, ruling folks, will go to purge themselves to deflect the taint: I don't have a racist bone in my body, I didn't intend it, heartfelt condolences to the family, we are a nation of laws, we stand for justice, given our history how dare you suggest...

David Starkey (2011) denied that his blackening of white London looters in the wake of the Mark Duggan killing by police was *racial* stereotyping. He insisted he was characterizing culture not biology, in immediate self-denial about the long and deep histories of racial culturalization and culturalizing modalities of racial expression and racist exclusion, ridicule, and rationalization. The blissful state of ignorance, beyond and beside belief. Where individual racist expression is made an issue, the apology is invariably for the offense taken ("I'm sorry if you are offended"), almost never for causing offense, harm, or hurt. This, in turn, silently displaces the blame for the offense from the offender to those taking offense.

The postracial as condition thus is also a passage to reversals: of who gets charged with racism. The privileged charge the relatively disprivileged or the insurgent: Whites call blacks or Muslims racist. Israelis condemn Palestinians. The Democratic Alliance Party in South Africa point fingers at the ANC. Republicans in America charge Democrats, or claim historical credit for ending slavery as a way of denying their own implication in the institution (cf. David Barton's historical revisionism). Tea Partiers now dismiss any charges of racism by characterizing those charging racism as too thin-skinned to take a joke. The inheritors of historical racial privilege deny its racist expression, while insisting that its occasional occurrence is individualized to the isolated bad apple. At the same time, the morally rejected behavior of the racially disprivileged is rationalized as the expression of maligned group culture. Turnaround, it seems, is fair play. It is also in keeping with the political right's tactic to take over the terms of progressive critique and turn them against the commitments for which they have long been taken to stand. US conservatives, for example, have sought in the name of a "Civil Rights Initiative" to repeal progressive civil rights gains.

The social work of postraciality

The postracial, it follows, is not only a racism without race or a racism without racists (cf. Bonilla-Silva 2003). The language of race disappears, only to dis-appear, to appear elsewhere in terms no longer conventional and easily recognizable (Goldberg 2012). Rather, neoliberal postraciality amounts to "racisms without racism"

(Goldberg 2009). This is the enigmatic condition of the circulation of racisms, renewed, reinvented, resurrected, born again though never dead, without the terms to name it as such, to identify, comprehend, or condemn. We could even call this racisms' avatar condition. It reduces to singularity what is plural, poly-expressive, and pluri-conditional. Rendered as *the* postracial, raciality is homogenized to the monotony of mono-expression, to be dismissed more readily. *This* too is the *enterprise* in neoliberalism's postracial condition.

The "post" in the putatively postracial accordingly references the afterlife, the ghostly haunting by the racial of the social supposedly rid of race. To be putatively postracial is to imply, if not to admit, that the society in question must have been inscribed by race. But the implication of raciality is not quite admission, indeed it implies a denial of its once and present racism (cf. Wise 2009). Postraciality effectively erases any record of raciality. The postracial, then, is racial as spirit condition of the social, sociality's unnamed because unnameable spirit, its shadow being. The postracial is another modality of racially marked and racially exclusionary sociality (in denial, and in denial of that denial).

Postraciality is committed structurally to expanding new markets and the identities to support them emanating from but exceeding traditional expressions of raciality. As a means to expansive marketization, postraciality assumes a master thread in the social fabric of neoliberalization. Markets are encouraged or expanded by seeking out new mixtures and "the middle ground" (Hall 2011) they presuppose and (re)produce. Neoliberalizing postraciality's "meeting in the middle" extends renewed energy to integration as postracial expression, effectively leaving in place long-established hierarchies of racial (re)structuring.

The postracial accordingly is the predictable elaboration of the neoliberal through unleashed and unlicensed social intercourse and mixtures. Almost but not quite anything and everything goes. Mimesis, or mimicking imitation, is evidenced in the insistence that the standards, values, and social conditions to be aspired to and emulated are those of the racial dominant, of whiteness as transparent condition. This transparency allows the thick traces of racial privilege to be penetrated only by mimicking dominant sensibilities. Where mimetic mixing breaks down, where rogues and rogue states erase the securing boundaries of socially acceptable mixture, recourse to institutionally mandated violence is invoked.

Neoliberalism and its neo-neoliberal hyper-extension drive a wedge between the spheres of the state, economic, and civil society. The emphases on robust economic deregulation and privatization, combined with intensified social re-regulation (Hall 2011) and the independence of an expansive private sphere, are deployed to produce multiple effects. They work to curtail the impact of the state and its regulatory apparatus designed to expand equity, shrinking the power of government over economic matters. Political power is either ceded or redirected in favor of extending economic power and social capital. These emphases have been coterminous with the perception that government and its apparatuses have become increasingly diverse, if not black, less controllable as a consequence by traditional (and overwhelmingly white) elites.

In the wake of the 1960s, the state came increasingly to be identified by conservative critics with welfare and the license of racially insinuated if not identified criminality. The emergent commitment of the neoliberal state, by contrast, was to shift from social security to an expanding state security apparatus. This was a response to the growing fear of black power and to white insecurity, and was manifest in a defunding of the welfare superstructure and a dramatic enlargement of the penal state, in the rendering of employment more flexible and less secure. The neoliberal state makes the precarious invisible, including those lacking work, needed skills, and capital, increasingly warehousing them in prisons (cf. Wacquant 2009). The accompanying turn to the rhetoric of the postracial erased critical analysis, transforming the seemingly "Invisible Man" of the 1930s, 1940s, and 1950s (Ellison 1952) into the "Invisible Condition" of the post-1980s. This invisible condition is one of ready disposability of anyone not white or white-like and self-responsible. It dis-appears those lacking use-value, (seemingly) belonging to a disturbing category, or threatening the immunology of the privileged nation-state and its body politic.

Postracial animalization

Recourse to animalizing representation has long served to dehumanize populations that are not European or supposedly of European descent. Beastliness underpinned the refusal of sovereign self-determination in the interests of exploitation, even to the point of disposability, so long as there were more who could be pressed into exploitable service. Consider the extreme case of the Congo Free State at the turn of the twentieth century, where Belgium's Leopold II oversaw the extermination of 10 million people to produce profits from the rubber trade. To animalize is to undercut the autonomy necessary to self-determination. It erases reason as the grounds for self-directing decision-making and, by extension, the political sovereignty necessary for self-rule. What ramped up in the twentieth century was the recourse to animalization in producing and rationalizing group extermination (to the point of extinction) of the unwelcome and the threatening. "The problem will be solved if we can just get rid of the termites."

In undercutting any possibility of self-determination, racial animalization has been selectively invoked more recently to warrant delimiting state support and refusing state dependence in the form of social welfare. As black and brown populations grew in numbers or power in societies hitherto considered white(-controlled), the caretaking state came under increasing attack. Both the neoliberally manufactured dwindling of state resources for caretaking and the explosion of state commitments to "homeland security" have been justified in the name of animalization. It has been mobilized in establishing "welfare queens," "terrorist organizations," and "rogue states." Disposability in the forms of abandonment, externalization, disappearance, invisibility, incarceration, or, more extremely, extermination has been enabled in part by the resounding rhetorics of low-grade animalization: rats, termites, cockroaches, snakes, sheep, and so on (Derrida 2011; Mavhunga 2011).

Other species of animal higher in the chain of being – skunks, moneys, baboons, orangutans – are invoked more as analogies than as literal identifications. They operate mostly as expressions of humiliation rather than as stepping-stones to disposability. They are degradations, to be sure, racially prompted devaluations of humanity, but less as the mortifying calculations of the exterminator than as the infantile hostilities of the playground bully. (The identification of Ebola as originating in the passing from monkeys to West Africans is the exception here, as evidenced by a recent *Newsweek* cover [Edwards 2014].) In the end game of disposability with regard to populations deemed terrorist, socially valueless, or incapable of self-responsibility, the rhetoric employed invokes animals restricted to surfaces and subterranean existence, the bearers or transmitters of viral dis-ease. They are defeatable and disposable, so to speak, only by boots on the ground (here Ebola is no exception).

The postracial condition today, then, employs these variously instrumentalizing racial animations while denying they add up to racism. Or denying indeed that racial characterization is being invoked. And denying that denial. In calling Gazans snakes, not only do Israelis deny any racial reference. They swat away the denial as unworthy even of momentary consideration. This postracial condition has been made a default mode of globalization's neoliberalizing political rationality, the seams of its social logic and cultural expression.

The postracial thus cuts away (from), undercuts, or discredits the terms for identifying, analyzing, and addressing racially charged distinctions and discrepancies. Postraciality increasingly erases or erodes the possibility of identifying racisms and their underpinnings, their structures and implications. It substitutes for all of this the disposition of a generalized disposability or containment of anyone taken to threaten the immunity of the body politic. Hence the proliferating emphases on animalization.

Postracial reversibilities

In removing the terms of racial analysis, the postracial also undercuts any capacity to account for their conditions of possibility and historical emergence, and so also their delimitation. The postracial, accordingly, ends the possibility of *seeing* racisms and their structures of enablement, their conditions of possibility. It makes of the racial a see-through or a see-past condition, transparent and transitory (Mitchell 2012).

Postraciality, then, blinds us to the racial, to racisms, their materializations and traces. Barack Obama, Republican Senator Tom Coburn insisted, is "a wonderful man ... I just have a lot of admiration for him." But as "an African-American male," Coburn continued, he "received 'tremendous advantage' from government programs ... his intent is to create dependency because it worked so well for him" (Sargent 2011). The postracial President is marked with racism in the name of friendship ("some of my best friends are ... "), while race is explicitly evoked (African Americans, affirmative action) and yet there is a silencing of the possibility of calling it for what it is. As a friend he is like me, only not. He is distantiated by subtle differentiation; put to (political) death by dislikening, in the name of liking.

As this example attests, the postracial quite implicitly insists on reversibility (cf. Norton and Sommers 2011). Fox News commentator Jonathan Hoenig during a discussion bemoaning the widespread concern that race was a driving factor in the Michael Brown killing blurted out, "You know who talks about race? Racists ... " Racial reversibility involves the insinuation that those targeted by racist expression and practice are actually the ones responsible for having perpetrated racial wrongdoing in the first place. The Fox News program, oddly, was exactly discussing race, which on their commentator's criterion makes them racist. The Fox insinuation is not that any talk of race counts, but only left-critical talk. President Obama was capable of his achievements just by being dependent on the unfair advantages of affirmative action unavailable to whites. As Auster insists, "If postracial America does not mean the removal of... pro-nonwhite, anti-white policies and beliefs, what does it mean? It means a post-*white* America, an America transformed by the symbolic removal of whiteness as the country's explicit or implicit historic and majority identity" (Auster 2008). The horror, the horror.

Comparably, if in a different context, Newt Gingrich, frontrunner for the Republican Presidential election nomination in 2012 at the time he uttered these words, declared Palestinians to be "an invented people." Lacking a state, they are generic Arabs, who could and do live anywhere, and so have no claim on "Israeli" territory. Now, if statehood is a condition of peoplehood, pretty much every "people" is invented at some point. Defending his claim against the predictable criticism, Gingrich further demonized the Palestinian people as having been politically fabricated only in 1977: "They are all terrorists," he declared in an Iowa primary debate (December 10, 2011). Judging from the reaction, no one noticed or seemed to care about the generic – if not genetic – reversibility.

These reversals – no longer the domain of the white privileged and powerful but supposedly of the black and brown ("unfairly") advantaged – are underpinned by a more general resonance. Racism loses its historical legacy; anyone can now be racist. Writing about the popular American television program *30 Rock*, philosopher J. Jeremy Wisnewski (2010: 58) commented that "As hard as we try to avoid it, we may harbor racist assumptions – no matter what color we are." Formal equality trumps even the deepest (and formally produced) substantive inequality. And if the historically disadvantaged, disenfranchised, and disempowered today are readily racist too, racism must be no more than the sort of traffic infraction we all engage in repeatedly and no one bothers to call out.

The postracial thus inures us to how racisms feel, to the affective implications of racisms' expressions. Self- and socially licensed to say publicly anything that comes to mind about blacks or immigrants of color or Muslims or migrants generally, public figures in any presumptively majority white society have expressed themselves openly in perniciously prejudicial terms. They appear indifferent to the harm their contempt may cause, to the violence or discriminatory exclusions they may encourage directed at members of the targeted racial groups. In Orange County, California, white Christians have made Muslim women and children run a gauntlet of ugly crowd epithets just to shop at the supermarket or visit the doctor. Geert Wilders, the Dutch parliamentarian renowned for his insults of Muslims, has repeatedly equated the Qur'an with *Mein Kampf*, with little formal admonition (or without acknowledgment that *Mein Kampf* was born of a European drive to rule the world). The Dutch high court cleared Wilders of any wrongdoing, upholding his free speech rights (though he is now being recharged for inciting violence).

The postracial makes it possible to ignore, avoid, or fail to attend to the spiraling disparities between the deraced privileged and the racially de-faulted disprivileged (in short, the racial default). So the postracial becomes not just the cover-up, the ideological "racializing" rationalization after the fact. It is the constitutive ordering that enables extension of the disparities from the racial default. Not only do blacks remain poor, the poor are made to be black. As David Starkey remarked, "Britain's white looters became black." And for Newt

Gingrich, only blacks are the beneficiaries of food stamps.

The postracial thus reinforces claims to a racial ontology, to racial being-in-the-world, by purporting to render race itself ontological. It is made the unremarked and unmarked given of Being, of nature. It is simply a transparent and so taken-for-granted fact of life as such, from which there is then no escape. The race-ing of Being is the being of Race. Race in the making is, tautologically, the making of race, its more or less guaranteed social delivery. The new genetics of race exemplifies this ontologizing of race. Various critics have demonstrated that the genetic "discovery" of racial traits or racially associated diseases is already implicit in the studies' epistemological assumptions (Fullwiley 2011; Abu El-Haj 2012). The manifestations are rendered invisible, see-through, deniable because virtually traceless.

The postracial, accordingly, embeds an epistemology of deception. Things are not as they appear to be. The nonracial, to which postraciality is conceptually wedded and out of which historically it has grown, is the refusal to acknowledge the structures of race ordering the social. In denying racial structures, in assigning them to an unreachable past, all the while devaluing the extent of their lasting effects, postraciality fails – really refuses – to comply with or to live up to pre-ordained expectations about how racial configuration and racist expression manifest: slavery's emancipation was brought about by Republicans; the black US President is committed to enlarging racial dependency for African Americans; profiling Muslims as potential terrorists is demanded by state security; Muslim-American students peacefully disrupting in civil protest the Israeli Ambassador's rationalization of Gaza's invasion turn out to be violating his free speech rights and disturbing the peace.

Deception operates as a logic of tactical calculability in the face of uncertainty. It is not that postraciality reshuffles the structural deck. Rather, it deceptively enlarges and deepens the modes of articulation, expression, rationalization, and explanation of its extended racialities. It doubles down on their impacts and refusals while seeking to obscure from view their racial significance and extension.

The postracial, in the final analysis, is a mode of social magic: the alchemy of racism into nonracialism, into deracination. It sacralizes the negation in the name of desacralizing anti-racist struggle. It etherealizes racisms in the spirit of *its* overcoming. The ghosts of racisms past are dissolved into the indiscernible pixels making them up.

Postraciality's con-fusions

Recourse to the postracial holds at arm's length, though just barely, the threat of conceptual confusion. Confusion concerns here the conflation or mixing of categories accompanying the massive demographic movements of globalization and the associated stress on mixtures, commercially and culturally. Mixture and mash-ups constitute the objects of contemporary desire and practice. The postracial articulates the refusal of the world's dissolving mixings. It expresses the fear of being confused, of mixing one's metaphors, of misstating because misreading who one is speaking to, for, about, and against. Call this, following Alex Abramovich (2009), the fear of being "phenomenologically fucked." The postracial seeks to stave off the conditions of being conceptually perplexed: Is she, isn't she? It is the perennial paranoia now of being phenomenologically screwed (up).

Far from being a thing of the past, racism has become reanimated as a key instrument of the political, only now in new ways and to novel purpose. That the notion of race can be so easily filled with new political purpose is basic to its flexibility and politically instrumental nature. A strategy of raciality – and here postraciality is no exception – seeks to extend *suspicion* to anything marked by its terms, effectively to erode the standing of those racially inscribed by innuendo or more explicitly. Postraciality serves in principle and fact to refuse, often violently, any mixing that threatens to challenge the status quo, to dilute its givens, to undo its presumptive purity. Those supposed not to belong or to threaten by virtue of their nonracial raciality are considered to embody suspiciousness, to be suspect in the very condition of their being (Levinson 2014).

All those who are not white, but blacks especially – in the United States without question but anywhere whites rule – are the object of suspicion. Recall the revival by Thatcher's government in the 1980s of Britain's century-old "sus laws" to target young black men on city streets. This has a long racial history. In the neoliberalizing turn to securitizing conditions for capital, its power brokers and possessors, the conditions promoting suspiciousness have heightened. Walls have gone up, both state- and individually sponsored, supplemented by technologies of surveillance and deadly fortification (Goldberg 2013).

In the latter half of 2014, American police killed black people with alarming regularity, whether walking in the street, engaged in small if sometimes illicit enterprise to get by, shopping, or even at home. A 25-year-old woman with her three-year-old daughter was accused of shoplifting at a WalMart in suburban Georgia. As she left the building she was confronted by a police officer who ordered her to the ground. On her knees she reached into her pocket for her cell phone and was shot dead by three bullets before the terrorized eyes of her child. Another motherless daughter. To admit that no shoplifted merchandise was found on her, while reinforcing her innocence, undercuts the admission by implying that were she guilty of shoplifting, killing her would have been proportionately just. A seven-year-old black girl asleep on the sofa aside her grandmother was killed by a single police bullet when police raided the wrong Detroit apartment to arrest a criminal suspect. Another (grand)daughterless (grand) mother. In Pontiac, Michigan, a policeman stopped a young black man literally for walking with his hands in his pockets against the snowy cold (Alter 2014). As Sara Ahmed (2014a) has remarked, police kill unarmed black people because they are deemed weaponized in virtue of their blackness. Barely obscured by postraciality, police suspicion quickly turns deadly when one is not white. Postraciality heightens as it (barely) hides black death, the law of racial elimination (Rankine 2014).

In the wake of violent police response to community protests in Ferguson, much has been made of militarizing American police forces. One can point to similar concerns in South Africa, France, Britain, and elsewhere, almost invariably in response to street resistance by angered youth of color. In Gaza, it has been insisted by an Israeli military spokesman, not only are there no civilians, but all residents are under suspicion of terrorism or its support. Gazan adolescents playing on the beach seeking release from military bombardment become fair game (Mullen and Wedeman 2014).

If suspiciousness is the ontological condition of the targeted, militarization is now the condition of the racially self-empowered. The notion of "martial races" is not new. In the 1920s and 1930s, some British military officers sought in India and Africa to identify those "native" groups more inclined to qualities deemed necessary for military service and more readily identified with Northern European manly virtue: courage, trustworthiness, strength in body, character, and judgment (MacMunn 1933; Streets 2004; Goldberg and Giroux 2014: 123–4).

What is new today about the martial spirit is not the identification of some natives to supplement the colonizing powers in the conduct of European or global wars. Rather, it is the establishment of a heightened martiality for the sake of unquestioned control, establishing and maintaining absolutized sovereignty especially over racially identified populations. This includes the aggressive show of force, violent confrontation, generic suspicion, and anonymous detention without trial.

In the United States after 9/11, the Department of Homeland Security funded police departments to acquire significant military weaponry, such as surveillance drones, armored military vehicles including tanks, full combat body armor, gas masks, grenade launchers, and M-16s (Balko 2013; Greenwald 2014). The nominal rationalization is anti-terrorism preparedness. In fact, equipment intended for armed combat in desert terrain has been operationalized for routine drug raids in (sub)urban America. But militarized police force has been mobilized also to quell urban protest, from the Occupy movement to citizens concerned about police violence, and not only in America. Police forces have been encouraged to become paramilitary forces, as the responses attest in Ferguson and London in the wake of Michael Brown's and Mark Duggan's killings by police, in the *banlieues* of Paris, and in trade union strikes at the Marikana mine in South Africa.

Militarized strategy and tactics worked out in racially re-shaped sites such as Gaza, Iraq, and Afghanistan get re-imported into and fused with policing metropoles. Just as sites with an enduring history of colonial racism are the prompting conditions for such weaponry, so racially produced and shaped urban and strategic sites – long policed by helicopters at night – become the grounds for experimenting with and "perfecting" para-militarized policing at home.

Increasingly in American cities, police shoot black men, women, and children, many within seconds of arriving, and without warning. They often fabricate after the fact the "threatening" conditions they claim gave rise to the shooting. It was a police officer, not peaceful protestors, who declared in Ferguson that "I will fucking kill you," while another loudly insisted "I will fuck you up." In Gaza, leaflets were dropped by Israeli military in densely populated areas giving residents three minutes to vacate their residences before bombs were dropped on their heads. Suspect populations and traumatized, angry officers trained to kill are the triggering mechanisms for itchy-fingered martial personnel frustrated at challenges to their authority. Postraciality places the boot – albeit a brittle glass one – squarely on the foot of the politically powerful.

All this makes evident that longstanding, if subtly transmuting, racial orders invariably shadow the post-racial, constitutively delimiting its possibilities and con-straining its reach. Structurally, postraciality maintains prevailing conditions of historically produced racial arrangement and power, both domestically and globally, now stripped of their historically inherited terms of recognizability, address, and redress. Ideologically, postracialism (the discursive formation representing the combined conditions of the postracial characterized here) does not solely absolve whites of guilt for past racisms. Rather, it erases the very histories producing the formations of racial power and privilege, burying them alive but out of recognizable reach. They wipe away the very conditions out of which guilt could arise. That denial of denial: there is no guilt because there is nothing recognizable to be guilty about, least of all the guilt itself.

One finds this in the drive to rewrite school history books, in Texas among other states. Slavery is intentionally erased as an enforced and exploited condition in favor of characterizing it as the "Atlantic triangular trade." Any reference to the buying and selling of slaves in America is denied. Another change sought to describe the civil rights movement as "establishing unrealistic expectations of equal outcomes" among those not white (the changes, made in 2010, were overturned two years later by a less instrumentalizing new School Board). And yet a world history textbook mandated by the state still insists that "South of the Sahara Desert most of the people before the Age of Explorations were black

Africans of the Negro race," thus reinstating nineteenth-century racial classifications (Wray 2014). These Texan efforts are part of a larger, indeed global, postracial revisionism concerned to rewrite the histories of slavery as largely benign towards slaves, and colonialism and apartheid as mostly beneficial to the subjugated.

Anger among African Americans directed against the police bubbled over in Ferguson in the summer of 2014, after Michael Brown was killed by a local white policeman. Ferguson's approximately two-thirds black residents are policed by a fifty-three-person police department employing only three black men. The mayor and city council, but for one exception, are white, as too are nearly all the business owners. Poverty in the suburb has doubled in the past decade, almost exclusively among the black residents. Twenty-five percent of blacks, while just 11 percent of whites, live below the poverty line. Across the country, poverty rates increased by 36 percent overall. In suburbs, where people are locked into lack of opportunity, poverty increased by 64 percent, driven mostly by the racial poverty rate. The black unemployment rate in St Louis County remains double that of whites. In Ferguson (part of that county), it is almost 20 percent, three times the white rate (Wiltz 2014). Black drivers are stopped by police and arrested at twice the rate of white drivers, even though the contraband found in vehicles driven by whites and blacks is pretty much equivalent.

In the name of postraciality, racisms are manufactured and manifested more silently and informally. They are expressions of private preference schemes rather than of formalized state policy. They reproduce and cement in place as givens of nature the racial orders of the prevailing social structure. The "Anthropocene" is not just the geologic time in which humans intervene in nature but the time – our time – in which humans make nature. The anthropocenic understands nature as now also the product of human creation so that the last frontier has been reached, the final barrier breached. In anthropocenic terms, the postracial amounts to the admission (at long last) that the racial is not a natural category. Rather, it is made and remade no longer largely by the state but by human beings in the tactical calculations of their self-advancement and retention of their capacity to ensure their competitive prevailing.

The postracial accordingly is a product and representation of the drive to control the elements to ultimate competitive advantage. The *anthroporacial* (to coin a term) represents racial arrangements as anthropo-divine design. It is a human re-creation projected as if divine intervention. The postracial accedes sovereign authority – for criteria of merit, advancement, and value – to those long established as carrying racial weight but now shorn of explicit racial reference or responsibility.

The postracial, it could be said consequently, confuses the human with the divine. It is not just that the human aspires to divinity but it takes on the mantle of godly power. Postracialism (the modes of representing and seeking to legitimate postraciality), in turn, denies just how conceptually confused we have increasingly become, and how phenomenologically impoverished it actually leaves us. It hardens into place the structures of racially reproduced subjection. Postraciality (the set of conditions) and postracialism (the modes of representation) distressingly render us phenomenologically debilitated, over and over. And postracial militarization is an undertaking to fix these uncertainties by forcing categorization into and onto the unclassifiable.

Postraciality does not exist today alongside the conventionally or historically racial. It is not one expression of contemporary raciality among others. The postracial *is* the expression of raciality for our times, *tout court*. It has taken over. It puts to new uses, to novel applications and impacts as deemed fit, this or that of raciality's histories of instrumentalization and rationalization. In this, it is one with contemporary political economy's utterly avaricious and limitless appetites for the new. It makes new of the old. It readily discards and disposes, if not re-uses and remixes, without second thought whatever (including whoever as whatever) is taken not to comport with current designs. Hence the rhetorical fashion so ubiquitous today of the non-responsive response, "whatever..."

I turn in the following chapter to delineating the principal subjects constituted by these logics of post-raciality: the figures of "the Black," the "Muslim," "the Palestinian/Gazan," and "the Migrant." Their raciality is made, extended, remade by and in the name of postraciality.

FOUR

Postracial subjects

Postraciality amounts to a general social ecology within which race and racisms are supposedly outmoded but where, in fact, racist expression has gone viral. As with viruses generally, it is not that every social interaction produces a viral outbreak, an instance or circulation. Some are immune, some are conscious about avoidance and precaution, some previously infected have learned from the experience. Still others may circulate in parts of the landscape where the virus is less visibly active, and even remain relatively untouched by it. This does not preclude the possibility of its activation. An outbreak can occur at any moment. Segregated or firewalled social spaces may artificially diminish the prospects for a viral outbreak, much as less densely populated urban areas might delimit the likelihood of viral spread. But this hardly undercuts the conditions of possibility for an occurrence or more virulent circulation. So with postracial ecologies. Racist events are considered occasional, yet the postracial conditions of their possibility structurally enable their proliferation, even at epidemic levels.

Postracial ecology

Racism is not only about what one person does to another. Racisms are always expressed within a landscape of racially framed and structured conditions. They exist in an ecology of power relations and racial conceptions ordered by that landscape. So every racism is relationally structured. It is how those with power treat those with relatively less, within an established set of existing social orderings. These relations are reinforced by larger regional and global relations of historically conceived and contoured racial power. Identity commitments and ascriptions (black, brown, white, etc.) are not established in a vacuum, unrelated to larger landscapes of social relation. Racial arrangements and the social positions inhabited by those racially defined are always constituted through relational conditions of power and its articulations.

This obviously represents a contrasting account to the standard view that postraciality concerns the social irrelevance of racial consideration. This widely presumed irrelevance can be variously interpreted. A central insistence is the fading of any social traction of racial identities, arrangements, and considerations. Here postracialism is a claim, demonstrably misleading today, that racial determinations have lost all power, if they persist at all. Another reading of postracial irrelevance is to admit the persistence of racial claims while discounting their traction. Racial interests, it is insisted, (should) play no role in deciding the outcomes of moral, political, economic, or legal claims. The postracial accordingly is the rejection of any racial claim in favor of policies seeking nonracial, universal reach. It represents the latest version of classic liberal commitments (cf. Wise 2010).

Postraciality, additionally, would have us believe there are no more racial subjects. Far from just a normative claim, this is both a factual and an aspirational assertion. In the name of the aspiration, what in fact has materialized is less a tamping down of racial reference and racist assertion so much as a context-bound heightening of the raciality of some groups or subjects while rendering that of others (more) invisible. As the precarious have been made more so, their raciality has been (re-)emphasized. The terms of emphasis may have shifted, yet the rhetorics of representation, often linked to more conventional historical terms, take on a novel articulation and (re)new(ed) significance. Not a day goes by now without more or less contentious, often demeaning public reference to some or other aspect of black, Latino, Muslim, or Palestinian life.

Whiteness, by contrast, has been rendered less racially visible. In general, the traditionally racially powerful have shed the skin and skein of race. Their raciality has become more transparent, less on the sleeve, less obviously or visibly racial. The less powerful and more marginalized, meanwhile, have had their racial characteristics emphasized, heightened, made a badge of identification. They have been made hyper-visible, even as the *conditions* producing their precarity have been increasingly ignored by policy-makers and their powerful supporters. These conditions have become more socially invisible. So the postracial is the sociality of heightened raciality in the name of its denial. Race-claiming and antagonisms, racial fabrication and aggressions, racial insistence and violence have all intensified, while their agents refuse to acknowledge their impacts and implications.

The Anthropocene, I suggested in Chapter 3, represents the age of collapsing distinctions between the human, natural, and technological spheres, between agency and causal animation, subject and object (Latour 2014). With these distinctions blurring, if not disappearing completely, the lines between them can no

longer be discerned. Not only are humans now inter-
vening in natural forces to cause significant shifts in
natural conditions, such as global warming, dramatic
polar melts, sea-level rises, and so on. The human and
technological interventions regarding the natural, and
the techno-human remaking of nature, are now producing natural-human changes. Such changes, in turn,
are impacting the future of human *being*, the conditions
and *nature* of the human. They have also prompted a
renewed stress on geneticizing race (call this "gene-
race," or "re-gene-race").

These collapsing distinctions are affecting also how
racial consideration impacts the social. I have stressed
already the renewed streak in cultures of degradation to
animalize people. In one direction the anthropocenic
interpenetration of the human and natural has prompted
the critical ontology of "the new animism" (Latour
2009; Viveiros de Castro 2012) as well as concerns
about species discrimination and treating animals
human(e)ly. In a counter-direction, though, it has
eroded much moral resistance to reducing humans to
(lower forms of) animal life. With the erasing of distinctions between categories of the human, natural, and
technological, there is a heightening impetus to characterize the non-belonging, the rejected, and the alienated
– the enemy, the dangerous, the threatening – as

unrecognizably human. As digital sensors are implanted in almost everything (the "internet of things"), things have increasingly become personified. Likewise, as animals acquire spirit, animalization of certain classes of people has re-ignited.

Animalized classes of people are demeaned as the most despised beings of the natural world, at least in dominant Western narratology: as vermin, insects, cockroaches; as rodents, snakes, maggots (Mavhunga 2011). The film *District 9*, set in post-apartheid South Africa and drawing on the segregationist history of apartheid and its aftermath, pursued these anthroporacial viralities in some depth. Video games likewise often exploit such racial imagineering as the inspirational source for their most sordid villains. Rodents – even cuddly ones like rabbits – are culled when too numerous, a nuisance. Nuisance and threatening people – the parasitical, the terrorist, the enemy, the unclean, the pestiferous – are likewise to be culled. Consider the carpet bombing of the Gaza "haircut" (ARRSE 2014).

It is not just animals generally but the *lower* forms of animal that now are to be exterminated, or at least thinned out – those closest to the ground, squirming on or under it, bearers of disease and dis-ease. Domesticated animals are to be loved, cuddled, succored, their expressiveness enjoyed. Pestiferous and parasitical ones are to be hunted out, or at least kept in check, because they always reproduce too fast to be killed off completely. Kill all Palestinian mothers, Israeli Knesset member Ayelet Shaked declared, to avoid reproducing new generations of Palestinians. All too few so much as murmured in critical condemnation.

Postracial conditions differ from those previously constituting raciality. At heart, the driving terms evidencing the structural underpinnings of racial articulation have been rendered less apparent, if not erased. Accordingly, racial arrangements and their structures of possibility become less obvious. This, in turn, implies that racist expression seemingly becomes only an occasional occurrence. Herman Cain, unsuccessful Republican Presidential candidate in 2012, expressed this precisely: "...the two incidents, one in Ferguson, Missouri [Michael Brown], and one in New York, Staten Island [Eric Garner], are two separate incidents representing exceptions rather than the rule...race relations in America as viewed through these incidents are not indicative of the real race relations in America that people find in their neighborhood and their community" (Cain 2014).

Racisms accordingly are taken to express themselves only in outbreaks (Valayden 2013). The postracial stands for racial outbreaks seemingly disconnected from each other. The possible grounds for identifying a relational structure commonly sourcing such expression have been made opaque. The terms of their relationality are erased.

Irruptive racisms

If racisms are anomalous in this scheme of things, they amount to tears in the social fabric rather than threads or materializations of its nature. Outbreaks are discrete, and indiscriminate. They are predictably unpredictable. They reinforce the sense that the society is constitutively healthy, not ravaged by the racial, yet more or less vulnerable to its diabolical irruptions and ruptures. What in fact is at work here is the restructuring of the conditions of racist expression, and their terms of articulation. It is not that the social has purged itself of the structures reinforcing racial articulation so much as that those re-articulated structures have been rendered more see-through and slippery.

This sense of outbreak as viral illness continues to imply that racisms are anathema to modern social order. In fact, racisms help to constitute and so are crucial to modern state-making. States become modern – are drawn into the modern world order – in good part by being conceived and conceiving themselves in racial terms (Goldberg 2002). Social structure dramatically shifted following World War II, with increasing speed and impact from the neoliberalizing 1980s onwards. Racial re-articulation followed suit. As formalized segregation gave way to growing civil rights access and creeping integration, and as post-apartheid and multi-culture revealed an increasingly diverse social ecology, racisms did not disappear. They morphed. Reacting to these newly articulated social arrangements, racisms were reshaped.

There is another sense to the conception of "outbreak" that more readily conveys this centrality of racial re-articulation to contemporary state formation. In addition to the notion that outbreaks are attacks on the social organism's health, they are also *skirmishes* between not just rival factions but also contesting states. Skirmishes suggest social battles, with the accompanying antagonisms both prompting and reinforced by the relations of contestation, mistrust, alienation, and violence inherently involved. Skirmishes are the momentary expressions – the outbreaks or outbursts – of already existing dispositions of aggression towards those considered the non-belonging. More often than not these skirmishes are triggered by inflaming circumstances in heated moments. As globalization sought to open up markets and movements, and as imaginary boundaries gave way to the romance with borderlessness, local populations became alarmed at disruptions by the fast-moving and alien. State borders hardened as claims to national self-definition and sovereignty reasserted themselves in the face of their sometime challenge.

Skirmishes erupted in this cauldron of reassertion and contestation. They are ready implications – really expectations – of society's increasingly militarized culture both in their technologies of control and in the underlying constitution of their social and civic order. Racial skirmishes between already established racial groupings or sub-groupings in established racial orders are spasmodic outbursts in the ongoing "race wars" or generally articulated class struggles (Foucault 2003). Here racial skirmishes are part of the open-ended struggles over power, the drive to establish and extend authority over those taken to buck or contest it. But they are also a desperate recourse to shore up status and social strength long predicated on racial arrangements in the face of social conditions eating away at or challenging them.

These skirmishing outbreaks thus represent struggles to sustain socio-racial power in socialities where that power is increasingly fought over. They reinforce the insistent drive to social militarization: individual gun ownership; foreign wars to cement regional or global power; militarized policing to solidify borders and boundaries; proliferating separation and securitizing walls to maintain local and personal control. They trade on long-established, if renewing but also increasingly see-through or evaporating, racial arrangements constitutive of social order. And yet, as outbreaks, they likewise project a sense of social anomaly, of non-ordinariness. The everyday and expected parade as the state of exception. And the explicitly unsaid and unstated become the easily deniable. Such is the "nature" of postracial racisms.

Skirmish culture also reveals that the modern imagination is saturated with militarization. Militarizing formulations infuse its categories and concepts, its forms of order and organization, meanings and metaphors, its very system of being and regime of truth, its cultural expressions and fashions. As such, the modern state's dance with death is no accident. It is not simply the externality of collateral damage, however rationalized. It is part of, for some even central to, its defining condition. Perhaps perpetual war, not the Enlightenment's perpetual peace, has become the very being of contemporary statehood, its raison d'être. War here is taken not only in its narrow sense of a time-bound battle. It signals every battle or struggle to the end, every violent confrontation, literally and otherwise. As Foucault (2003) puts it, every antagonism, rivalry, confrontation, and struggle between individuals, groups, or classes is taken up as fights, small and large. In the United States, every major social policy becomes aggrandized as a war, as campaigns with strategies and tactics, interrogations and taking territory: wars on poverty, against drugs, between parties, culture wars, perversely even a war to end war.

"Un-raced" raciality, racisms without race and racism, in this conception, becomes a (if not *the*) principal modality for defining and identifying the threatening within and without: the sub-human or sub-standard human, the beastly, the inferiorized, the deviant, the degenerate, the immature, even the (potentially) ill, from whom (from which), as Foucault reveals, society must be defended. Scrubbed of its pernicious historical resonances, the racial is sublimated within the intersections of more socially agreeable references. These include ethnic and national configurations long serving as racial media, if not surrogates. The military and police are institutionalized as the first lines of defense against the barbarians and beasts at the gate and within – from the inferior to the immature, the deviant to the criminal. The military defend against the socially threatening from without, the police from those within.

It has become increasingly evident that those lines between the interior and exterior, homeland and foreign land have been blurring too. The military and police – the militarized police and a policing military – serve against all those, the (raceless) sub-races, the animals, from which the extended homeland must purge and purify itself. The "Tau sub-races" in the fantasy game Warhammer exemplify the cultural imaginary in play here. Discourses, technologies, and rituals of "unracial" impurity and racial purification renew the insistence on social distinction from the animalized, the polluting, the non-belonging.

Militarizing postraciality

Militarizing modes of imagining are at the heart of how the contemporary postracial state now conceives itself. Militarization serves not just to protect belonging and secure social members in their insecurities from projections about the threatening outside. It equally operates to produce who belongs and does not. It is crucial to determining traitors both outside and in. The sorts of intelligence identified with and produced by militarization conjure cockroaches, rats, vermin, those posing as insiders that have to be unmasked as strangers, deviants, threatening "our" way of life. Militarization establishes how to identify who they are, revealing what threats they conjure, determining how best to manage them on the streets, apprehend, imprison, and annihilate them even in their expulsion.

The politics of postraciality demand such a culture of militarization. Militarization serves to extend racial identification and alienation as the explicit terms of racial reference are *dis*-appeared – eliminated without exterminating – and any racial significance can be denied when charged. Militarization thus drives a set of norms and values as well as a social analytics and understanding.

On the "homeland" side of alienation, alter-native, and alter(n)ation, militarization provides "substance" to national spirit. It colors its character(s) and pageantry, its performativity. It ordains something to be for, to be proud of, something "real" to which to commit, to fight for. This is a fight not just over principle or issue but for the sake of belonging itself. The military makes for feeling good about the collective self. Even the notion of national sacrifice through national service is medi-ated by the military, sublimated in its extended meta-phor. It serves up the first order of national commitment, demanding the giving of oneself, giving oneself, for the sake of the nation, taken as the ultimate sacrifice. In turn, warring's losses undercut national confidence. That failure of confidence projects a sense of compensatory bravado and aggression that more often than not intensifies the purging of the beastly and non-belonging.

In its expansive logic, wars and militarizing logic more generally collapse the distinctions between government, the military, and civilians or citizens. Citizens become conscripted, formally and informally. Yet they may be seen also as hiding, even shielding, militants. The distinction recalled from anti-colonial warfare or anti-apartheid struggle between freedom fighters and oppressors now becomes that between the legitimate military as protectors of the social and militants, terrorists, or enemy combatants as its threat. The collapse of distinction both reinforces and is reinforced by what is seen as a legitimate struggle and who in the asserted illegitimacy become legitimate targets: assassinating the other's politicians or leaders; carpet bombing the citizenry as one would the opposing military. "There are no civilians in Gaza," declared an Israeli general in the midst of Israel's blitzing of the territory. The collapse of distinction signals the collapse of limit. And in the collapse of both, the ultimate vulnerability of, threat to, and decimation of the political are made possible.

All this is done, more often than not, in the name of "defending civilization" and anxiously fighting for one's values from the position of "besieged civilized cultures" (Hage 2014). There are no longer centers and peripheries. There are only overlaps and intersections, barbarians circulating outside and inside the gates, walls, and boundaries, blurring the very lines themselves. The object of defense has shifted considerably from the nation as such to the *idea* of the nation (Demmers and Mehendale 2010). It transforms from the artifice of physical purity to the fantasy, the phantasm, of national homogeneity. In the expansive diversifications of globalizing political economy, postraciality helps to fashion a constraining national identity as homogenized polity.

Militarization offers a certain way for society to manage itself. Militarizing societies are those operating on particular projected presumptions of certitude in the face of radical uncertainty and its anxieties. It determines what is right, good, what actions need to be taken, how to respond. Risk is minimized, predictability absolutized, but only by expelling doubt, uncertainties, risk factors, either to the unthought or to the outside (Rumsfeld's various unknowns: Graham 2014). Militarizing societies tend to abhor critical interventions, let alone critical intellectuals. They produce "confirmatory" citizens. Citizens now confirm by repeating the standard line of a state allergic to criticism, "out of the box" thinking, or disconfirming counterfactuals. Globalization, ironically, has given rise to bubble cultures.

Postraciality assumes social homogeneity, producing local social universality, by alienating – literally rendering alien – the critical and disconfirming, the different and threatening. The non-conforming and non-confirming in being and behavior, culture and character are increasingly dealt with violently. They are excised from or refused entry to the body politic. They are rejected and ejected from social participation. This is found not only in the more obvious manifestations of military and militarized police "interventions" in local and global "hotspots," at least implicitly racially defined. It is evident also in the redefining of voter eligibility criteria and the homogenizing of voting districts in the United States.

These are longstanding racial instrumentalizations in establishing or extending political power. Yet, more often than not, they are predicated on well-established racial constitutions. What is novel about postraciality in all of this, as I have been arguing throughout, is the way it makes the racialities of such institutionalized violence, alienation, and excision paradoxically see-through and opaque, transparent and unseen.

The racial subjects of postraciality

Non-confirming and non-conforming social subjects are mostly racially identified, if not natally conceived and constituted. The prevailing racial subjects for postraciality are renewals, remakings, and mash-ups of much older racially fashioned subjects. These (re-) articulations produce novel identifications and representations. Blackness has always been basic to racist definition, and remains so with postraciality. The initiating focus on Arabs as one of the fifteenth-century European racial principals has become more broadly elaborated today. So Muslims and, in the specific context of Israel's politics, Palestinians (especially Gazans) have been mobilized as key racial subjects.

What may seem novel now is the way migrants are being racially identified and characterized. Here too there is a long tradition at work: consider East Europeans in late nineteenth-century London and New York, Mexicans and Asians migrating to work in California. The insistence that "migrant workers are taking our jobs," driving down wages, and polluting and devaluing neighborhoods are all charges with long histories. Today, as the state increasingly purges itself of explicit racial classification, there has been a novel renewal of bestialization, sewing together migration with the recent calculus around terrorism. While he was Texas Governor, Rick Perry insisted that ISIS terrorists may be entering the United States through the porous border with Mexico along with "illegal immigrants" (Wilkie 2014).

It follows, as Paul Gilroy (2010) has repeatedly argued, that both racisms and anti-racisms are fashioned in interactively global and local circumstances. Every racial place-time has produced its more or less specific racial subjects. Roughly, and in broad strokes, the earliest formulation and formation of racial subjects in the making of modern Europe included the Black, the Moor, and the Jew as non-Catholic and heathen interior aliens to be eliminated through conversion, expulsion, or extermination. New World Indians were established as exterior inferiors, savages of the state of nature. The Enlightenment largely produced Negroids, Mongoloids, Asiatics, and Caucasoids. The nineteenth century saw the identification of Negroes in more pernicious popular terms, and the state classification of Indians or Natives, with whites or Europeans as the driving category of domination. The twentieth century witnessed a proliferation of racial naming, and the hardening of demeaning, distancing, and deadly characterizations. As modes of racism came increasingly into question and societies grew more heterogeneous still, blackness stiffened into a variety of name-calling in different societies, each bearing comparable disparagement. Jews, Arabs, and Mexicans were likewise maligned to different if related political ends. The list could be expanded almost indefinitely.

Racial nonracials

Whiteness has been characterized as the defining power in the relational conditions of raciality. With postraciality, however, the incipient quality so basic to white as a racially defined subject position has seemingly evaporated. White has become the man without racial qualities. He (principally though far from only) establishes the standard of value. Invisible and transparent, he is the not quite absolute arbiter of power.

Once the defining character of powerlessness, and by extension blackness, invisibility now marks the white subject, the subject as white, of whiteness. Formerly the Invisible Man, blackness now stands for hyper-visibility. Not just hyper-visible, blackness is the very condition of hyper-visibility itself, of persistent suspiciousness and social marginalization. Like the sex talk parents inevitably face with their pubescent children, so black parents must face the "facts-of-black-life" moment, tutoring their children in how to negotiate the inevitable police stop. Black boys especially face puberty with the growing realization that they will live their lives repeatedly confronted by police, with potentially deadly consequence. Black innocence is placed in social question at these moments. White, by contrast, once absolutely visible, under postraciality has become (all but) completely transparent (cf. Dyer 1988, 1997). Historically the all-visible Sovereign, white now emerges into focus only in the outbreak racisms (in both the viral and skirmishing senses) of anxieties and cracking confidence.

Racism has always confronted black people first as black, and only secondarily, if at all, as human. Of course, being approached as black has shifted over time. However conceived, though, being considered black by those who are not invariably has meant being confronted *as* black, under the force of the associated meanings which have cast black people as less than fully human, assigning a caste character to them. Blackness accordingly implies less or other than human. Black life in a world defined, designed, and determined – given meaning – by those self-ascribed white is "fraught." It is at least in part agonizing, out of one's self-determination (Davids 2011). Under postraciality what differs for blacks is the denial that racism remains a concern. It is the refusal by the dominant that racism today has any impact, and the insistence that one is fully responsible individually for one's own social situation. (These are all characterizations Bill O'Reilly has pushed in repeatedly denying that white privilege persists.) Yet blackness, if less obviously, still bites hard today, socially, economically, and legally.

This racial "see-throughness" – a more or less new mode of dominant double consciousness – in turn enables, and perhaps ensures, that racisms will once again amplify violence. Racist violence has heightened precisely because it has been made less discernible, even unrecognizable, in so far as its objects are considered racially no longer to exist. "Free at last" takes on an altogether pernicious and threatening resonance for the dominant: self-entitled to say and do as a self-evaporating whiteness licenses. Whiteness here operates duplicitously in its transparency. Its openness prompts a heightening of veiled secrecy. Its erasures leave large social footprints and the contours of cultural affect. Far from being realized, central defining conceptions of critical anti-racism and civil rights commitment under postraciality have come to assume a far more sinister racial resonance.

The paradox of postraciality, then, is that its racial erasures are coterminous with new *intensities* in racist expression. This is more than correlation. The erasures have opened ways for the intensifications. These racial erasures have made racist expression seem less continuous than episodic, less chronically persistent than proliferating outbreaks, waxing and waning with viral circulations and skirmishes. Racisms here come across as agitations and assertive aggressions. The intensities of contemporary racist expression are attached to their outbursts. They are taken to dissipate, if not disappear, as the outbreak exhausts itself. Postracial racisms, accordingly, are deemed no more than episodic, nonstructural, without continuity, and so unsustained, even unsustainable. They are at one, in short, with racisms deemed anomalous, unusual, occasional, rather than sewn into the fabric of contemporary society.

It is curious that as racisms are thought to become anomalous, episodic, and occasional and are supposedly recessive, they have not only renewed their forcefulness. A heightened sensitivity has accompanied them and a prickly avoidability also. There has been a growing currency in public outings of racisms, especially in high-profile environments. I do not mean by this the common defensive concern among whites that black folk are constantly "playing the race card," nor the more counter-intuitive observation that somehow whites largely have become more critically anti-racist. Quite the contrary. Dominant organizations such as sports franchises and associations, media organizations, and universities all overwhelmingly tend to be under the control of white men. They increasingly find the need today to distance themselves from racist expression in their ranks. They nevertheless largely avoid addressing the generally invisible structural conditions usually under-pinning the racial tensions. Postraciality seems to have brought to the fore a cultural need to prove one's organ-ization is not racist by zealously distancing it from the episodic outbreak.

This suggests a more sustained culture of racist com-mitment underpinning the outbreaks. Taking distance from the particular episodic expression invariably leaves in place and unaddressed the underlying structural con-ditions that provide the conditions of possibility for such racist expression. It also obfuscates the relatedness, *qua* racist expression, of one outbreak to another. We cannot properly comprehend the proliferating images and expressions of black animalization politically and culturally, from video games to fashion magazines, without attending to their tissue of connection. The consequences are invariably violent, as borne out by the choking of an animalized black man by New York police for humorously challenging their authority by dancing in public (Agorist 2014).

Taken as a discrete anomaly, the callous police shoot-ing of Michael Brown was just another case of a fearful white policeman overreacting to a large black youth initially refusing to obey authority. But the shooting quickly revealed major structural underpinnings resonating more broadly throughout the country. The first, as I have argued above, is the militarization of policing in regulating mainly black and brown life. Police militarization exacerbates the disposition to use force. This recourse to force in turn is compounded by the well-documented shooter bias – "race on the brain" – increasing the likelihood of (especially white) police (like the broader public) shooting at black men. Most, but especially whites, more readily think that black rather than white men stereotypically bear weapons. Over the past thirty years, blacks in America have been twenty-one times more likely than whites to have been shot by police.

There is a second structural condition revealed by the Brown shooting. Mostly white municipalities in majority black towns across America have sought to raise significant revenue by collecting a slew of law-enforcing fees (Fausset 2014). So a traffic infraction will involve not just a fine but also a citation-filing fee charged to the transgressor. Failure to pay the fine and fee by a deadline will incur additional mileage fees for the police to serve papers on the defaulting person, associated court fees, and accumulated interest. A $100 fine can quickly balloon to $1,000. In jurisdictions where the proportion of white police officers in the force far out-weighs whites' proportion of the local population, black and brown drivers are twice as likely to be stopped by police as whites. They are more likely to be subjected to larger accumulated fines in part because they are poorer and unable to afford the fine in the first place, even though more contraband is found on white drivers. Not uncharacteristically, in Ferguson, a town of 21,000 people, two-thirds of whom are black, a staggering 33,000 citations were issued in 2013. More generally, budget woes due in good measure to tax cuts have decimated social programs. This has disproportionately impacted services to the racially defined poor. Post-raciality is invisibly squeezing to social death poorer black folk in a sea of social debt, who are then often effectively thrown into debtors' prison, or even the victims of utterly unwarranted deadly police shootings before they get as far as arrest.

I argued in Chapter 3 that suspiciousness attends to the social being of blackness. Simone Brown (2014) observes that the "fact of blackness," as Fanon (1968) put it, amounts to the long historical surveillance of black life. A constitutive condition of being black is the history of living under constant scrutiny: under slavery, Jim Crow, apartheid, CCTV, while shopping, driving, walking, by the criminal justice system, by society at large. Blackness, and those treated as if black – whether Irish and Jews historically or Palestinians today, for example – are allowed to live only by constantly being looked over: overlooked as they are intensely looked at, and socially dismissed. If for racially driven postraciality blackness is the condition of *criminal* suspicion, Muslims – usually identified reductively as Arabs – are taken as the embodiment of *political* suspiciousness and surveillance. And if a now depoliticizing violence can be said to be the everyday experience of blacks, a thoroughly politicized aggression is enacted against Muslim lives in non-Muslim majority countries.

Muslim-Gazan

In the United States, just under half the population today believes law enforcement ought to profile Arab and Muslim Americans (more than half of Republicans hold such views, believing also that such Americans are unfit to hold government employment) (Siddiqui 2014). In Israel, Arabs and Muslims – never distinguished – are widely maligned as Nazi-like in supposedly wanting to end Israel and all Jewish life. A form of self-defense, these widely held views among Israelis are predicated on characterizing all Arabs and Muslims as seeking Israel's demise as a Jewish state. North America and Europe inhabit a tradition defined as principally and presumptively white and Christian at their core (national prayers and houses of national worship today still bear this out). Muslims are taken not (fully) to belong. Their very presence is deemed menacing, challenging as it does the taken-for-granted homogeneity and presumed or desired purity of the national body. Increasingly from the 1980s, and exacerbated after 9/11, Muslims generically have come to be considered threatening, intolerant, in short, terrorists. From (multi) cultural contrast to existential threat.

Driving the image of the Muslim terrorist from the 1980s on has been the cut-out figure of the Palestinian, and in the past decade more specifically the Gazan. He, generically, is the suicide-bombing, rocket-launching, tunnel-digging, human-shielding manipulator. He is willing to sacrifice the lives of any and all, including his own family and children, for a religiously defined political cause. Such characterization is only sustainable by virtue of a triple repression: first, of the larger political and historical contexts of Palestinian subjection; second, of any humanness to Palestinians, and Gazans especially, in insinuating that they would so readily sacrifice their own immediate families, including children, women, and the elderly, to such an ill-defined political cause rather than struggling for a more peaceful existence; and, third, of any responsibility of the racially powerful in creating and extending the desperate conditions of Palestinians living life sentences of degradation.

There's a mind-numbing, often celebratory sensibility into which the processes of repressive violence sink. An Israeli observing the "Operation Protective Edge" attacks on Gaza in July 2014 publicly characterized watching them as "orgasmic." This signals exactly the tensions between the explosive deathly violence, the "orgasmic" eruptive "pleasure" of state-licensed spectacle and voyeurship, and the self-repressing burial of the ethical. The latter psychically makes pleasure by these means possible. Implicit here is the contrast between the alluring shiny weaponry at a distance – fighter jets, drones, awesome tank columns – of the US-supported Israeli military and the dirty, scrappy, resistance street-fighting amidst the crumbling infrastructure of bombed-out Gaza.

Refugee camps no longer suffice as holding pens. Their populations are increasingly superfluous, sewer people in the minds of their incarcerators, to be flushed out and away at every opportunity. They are little snakes, rats, or worms who should be left writhing headless and without any sense of direction. Refugees are no longer homeless, stateless, unfortunates. Indeed, they are no longer refugees but costly threats, with nothing left to lose, willing to risk their otherwise value-less lives by taking those of the self-righteous. Invisibil-ity, once a sufficient control strategy, has lost its cause. Only death will do.

As Gaza was being bombarded in July 2014, an Israeli woman embraced the driving racism of her society today: "We're racist because we want to preserve our lives and our sanity. So I'm proud to be a racist! If I'm racist in order to preserve my life, then I'm proud." The postracial racism fueling this discriminatingly indiscriminate bombardment was embraced as prideful Hobbesian self-preservation. In the shift from multicul-tural to postracial sociality, social responses to racisms have transformed from regrettable expressions to embracing racist practice as existential condition and disposition, as life-preservation. This expressive embrace of racist commitment is far from anomalous. The rabbi of an Atlanta suburban congregation, Shalom Lewis, sermonized on Rosh Hashanah that "Survival trumps all other issues in this war [against Islam] of values and decency." An Israeli man screamed at an Israeli woman publicly protesting the Gaza incursion: "You should be ashamed of yourself. You should be raped! Who are you married to? To a nigger. You have no shame. I'll stick a stick up your arse."

Shameless racist violence against the non-conforming is deeply intertwined with racially fueled violence against the considered enemy. Gazans are Israel's "kaffirs," their supporters (and Israel's critics) "niggers." In the reinforcing currents of relational racisms, Ethiopian Jewish women in Israel were unknowingly injected with a contraceptive drug to prevent them eugenically from diluting Israel's Jewish – which here can only be read as white, European – character (Chiles 2013). (In sporting and cultural contests, Israel competes in European leagues.) Following a judicial order releasing African asylum seekers from detention camps on grounds of the dignity of human life, a public crowd of Israeli adults led their grandchildren in chanting indignantly, "Niggers go home," "May you get AIDS, you daughter of a whore," "May you be raped, you whore," and the like (Diab 2014).

Maintaining the artifice of repressive purity is relational. The purging of Palestinians is at one with the female sterilizing and forced removal of Africans. Death-making requires the targets be visible; death at a distance renders the perpetrators opaque. Israel's more or less "raceless" social racisms are multi-directional.

They exemplify the violent extent reached by racisms purged of racism in their militant everydayness.

Connections between Gaza's and Ferguson's militarization, policing, and eruptions of the racist everyday highlight the postracial intensifications of contemporary racist expression. Such expressions are embodied and lived out in their explicit relationality. Ferguson police leaders were trained in security tactics by Israeli officals. A policeman in a town neighboring Ferguson posted on Facebook that Ferguson protestors should be "put down like rabid dogs...where is a Muslim with a backpack when you need them?" (Following the heated outcry, Officer Pappert was forced to resign [Murdock 2014], perhaps for violating the injunction of state racelessness.) More life-affirmingly, Palestinians tweeted to Ferguson protestors tactical advice in dealing with tear gas and stun guns (Hatmaker 2014; Khalek 2014).

Embedded here are reinforcing projections of black animals and Muslim terrorists. Under apartheid, all critics were deemed communist. Today, black boys are made criminal in virtue of their blackness. Likewise, postraciality transforms stone-throwing Palestinian kids protesting their spatio-political confinement into inevitable anti-state terrorists. In August 2014, John Crawford III picked up an airgun on sale at an Ohio Walmart.

The police were called and, upon entering the store, shot him dead without warning. Crawford, 22 years old and black, was not acting threateningly. In 2010, the Israeli military shot twenty-six Palestinian children in Gaza and the West Bank, killing eleven of them, most for stone-throwing.

Gazans, then, exemplify anthroporacial target subjects. Anthroporaciality is less the end of nature's independence, its auto-creation, than its human co-making pretty much all the way down. This means that racisms are not inevitable or expressive of some transcendental human nature. But it suggests also that their *supposed* inevitability – the self-licensing to purge a racially framed people as a "natural" entailment of human self-preservation – is politically projected in specific social contexts.

Anthroporaciality is not the older claim of inherent inferiority or superiority, nor one of historical immaturity. It is, rather, the assertion of "the new man" (Anthropocene's literal meaning) claiming natural self-preservation in the face of supposedly racially hostile threats. Postraciality's "new man" insists on self-defining and -refining his own destiny, making himself as he (re) makes his world. But he does so by necessarily denying the worlds of anyone antithetical to his world-making. He is, as a consequence, simultaneously paranoid and self-assertive, threatened and threatening, anxious and authoritarian, encircled and violently aggressive. In the deeply networked and interrelated globalities of movement and managed circulations, anthroporacial man has planetary designs and impacts. Anthroporaciality seeks inevitability for extended racist belittlement and exclusion, giving rise to while rationalizing them. Far from the end of racisms, anthroporaciality as postraciality's refining conception is their extended afterlife, renewed expression, and heightened violent manifestation.

Gazans especially have become the principally rejected by this new man, standing in the way of his world-making. Israel appears implicitly committed to fulfilling its theological premise of the "Promised Land" of "greater" or "complete Israel" from Eilat to Golan, the Mediterranean to the Jordan River. Gaza not only stands in the way of its fulfillment. It represents the human cost. Living in little more than a glorified ghetto or concentration territory, its residents can barely come and go. They exist on Israel's carefully calibrated and controlled subsistence diets, most of them under the meager poverty line. Israel has total control of the fenced and coastal perimeters, and almost total control of Gaza's air space, electrical grid, and water supply. All that seems under Gazan self-direction, strictly speaking, is its underground, criss-crossed by a maze of resistance tunnels created and controlled by Hamas under Israel's watchful gaze. Gazans, consequently, are seen by most Israelis as no more than underground snakes and worms. They are animalized tunnel diggers rushing to extend their tunneling into neighboring kibbutz kindergartens, murderous rocket launchers terrorizing Israel, circling vultures happy to project their own "telegenically dead children," as Prime Minister Netanyahu put it (Beinin 2014). Gaza and its global support hold in check Israel's reach for an expansive, purely Jewish state purged of Palestinians, even as it reinforces confirmatory Israeli citizenship. If for modernity race secularized the religious, anthroporaciality politically re-theologizes race.

Self-preservation is extended through these animations of violence and undercut in the animalization of those deemed threatening. When self-preservation is traded or substituted for generalized safety, those taken to count – both to be valued and to exercise the power of valuation – are narrowed to the legitimately living, members of the political community, in contrast to the living dead. In turning humans into wild animals, it is utterly predictable that the humans made animals, as Fanon (1968) observed with characteristic acuity, will bite back. And so they have, though more readily producing discomfort than existential threat, no matter the anxious fear-mongering to the contrary.

Anti-Semitisms are as old as Jews. They are prompted by different historical, social, and philosophical circumstances, assuming *racial* expression with modern Europe's coherence from the fifteenth century onwards. Today, alongside the indiscriminate and inescapable targeting of animalized Palestinians, sometimes vicious and deadly anti-Semitisms are recharging. In the name of a self-preservation the value of which is deeply bruised by totalized targeting of the dispossessed, the drive to destroy Gazans and delimit Palestinians' life possibilities re-prompts and reinforces anti-Semitisms by those incensed by their dehumanizing treatment. Anti-Semitisms worldwide, but especially in Europe, are reinvigorated against those perceived perpetrators and their supporters. (Hamas's own tactical violence, instrumental excess, and auto-immune anti-Semitism neither justifies nor fully explains Israel's morbid imperatives.)

Anti-Semitic outbursts throughout Europe, and most notably in France, have spectacularly increased the discomfort of European Jews. They include dramatic killings, synagogue and Jewish business burnings, and attacks on people, schools, and public sites like supermarkets, as evidenced by the disturbing *Charlie*

Hebdo events in Paris in 2015. While the rate of anti-Semitic incidents in France and Germany has been fluctuating wildly of late (Bittner 2014; Yardley 2014), their deadly spectacularity has dramatically increased. Anti-Semitisms both by disaffected, workless white youth and by young Muslim men – consider here the cartoonist and synagogue attacks in Copenhagen in 2015 – are fueled by an unforgivingness and fury in the face of extended futility and frustration, if for varying reasons. This makes their renewed expression no less problematic or painful for those objectified by and critically concerned about it. Far from blaming the victims or minimizing the effects of contemporary anti-Semitisms, this points to the relational quality of all racisms. Anti-Semitism (hardly the only or dominant racism in France today), Islamophobia, anti-black racisms, and anti-immigrationism are all of a piece (Fanon 1968: 86). European violence against Muslims, the long legacy of colonial histories, has outstripped anti-Semitic outbursts. Satirical caricatures of Muhammad (Cyran 2013), invariably unfunny, are no different than those of moneylending Jews (Sand 2015), black witchdoctors, or Gazan snakes. Addressing them relationally in terms of their intersecting sources and underpinning histories will likely undercut the prompts of the current outbursts, diminishing them to less consequential, though always unacceptable, expressions (Rose 2005).

The confidence of racisms in this new landscape is revealed to be a confidence trick. For postraciality, racisms can be thought in terms of an epistemology of deception. Here the cover of dust offers a counter-intuitively revealing mode of cover-up. Dust has long occupied the literatures, travelogues, and commentaries of modernity. It is overwhelmingly represented as the bearer of dirt and disease, contagion and the clogging of breath, pollution and threat to life. It obscures perception and clarity, covering over the dangers and disease of the unseen and the yet-to-come. Bourgeois interiors were to be daily dusted against disease. Today, travelers from the global North continue to comment on dust-covered street dwellers across the global South, threatening harm to and the health of unsuspecting passers-by.

Anxieties about dust and its relation to blood are succinctly captured by Walter Benjamin (2002: 104) in connecting between dirt, the diseased body, and militarized nationalist politics: "To give this dust a semblance of consistency, by soaking it in blood." Dust represents the polluted air of bombarded targets, behind which stand dust-encrusted bodies bled of life, lying in the rubble of blood-soaked streets and buildings.

143

This relation between deception and the dissolution of subjecthood suggested by the "dust people" (Dick 1954/1992) of inescapable bombarded sites prompts a rethinking of race as modes of deception, as the theological creation of peoplehood and its evolution. Race can be conceived in these terms as the secreting of identity, of distinction and contrast, in this doubled and ambiguous sense. It seeps into and molds personal, social, and political formation while also conjuring (public) secrets, even banalities, of belonging and belligerent banishment. Behind and beneath the dust, racial subjectivities dissolve in indistinguishability and indiscernibility, in paranoia and (imagined) threat, in the impossibility of identification and the collapse of distinction.

These racial complications around belonging are subtly revealed in the case of a lesbian couple who sued a sperm bank for "wrongful birth" and "emotional suffering" because, despite requesting a white donor, they were inadvertently provided "black sperm." The result was an unexpected mixed-race daughter. They claimed emotional distress resulting from their unpreparedness for bringing up a black child in a white family surrounded by white, conservative, small-town mid-America (Sharp 2014). The comforts of homogeneity collapse into the seething mass of heterogeneous swirl.

The traditional virtues of citizenship dissolve and disappear behind the dust of bombed territory, deserted borderlands criss-crossed by migrating dust people seeking out opportunity, more sustainable and safer lives. These dis-appearances, re-appearing in unpredictable places, are also dis-appointments, in at least two senses. They concern the dashed expectations as much by the necessarily failing forces of containment and securitization (consider the racial dynamics in white American responses to Ebola) as by those migrating with little left to lose often finding the gains illusory. And in the consequent dislocations they signal uncertain and unpredictable possibilities challenging the given and gatekeeping, the forces of delimitation and negating refusal. Dis-appearances and dis-appointment consequently lie at the heart of postraciality's racial renewals and renewed racisms. But they also signal improvisational outcomes, work-arounds, and make-overs. I want in the following chapter to identify with counter-traditions of the nonracial and the anti-racist.

Blacks and Gazans especially, Palestinians and Muslims more generally, are the renewed racial subjects of postraciality. *Migrants*, likewise long marked by race, constitute nevertheless a uniquely postracial subjectivity chronically dis-appearing and re-appearing.

The migrant

Dissolution of modern subjectivity, emblematic in the microbic molecules of dust, as Dick (1954/1992) so vividly conveys, is exacerbated in the late modern proliferation of geographies of walking. Migrant racialities are embodied in displaced subjects moved to traverse great distances. They seek to escape war, the effects of dramatically unsettling socio-natural disaster, anthropocenic dislocation, extreme economic difficulty, genocidal threats, and catastrophic political expulsions. Dust people are literalized and allegorized in the falling swirl of bombed buildings and long dirt roads, climatic storms and anthropocenic fields of fading dreams, in the dirty glitter of death-ridden mines and *maquiladora* sweat shops, in sex-, domestic and care work where serving involves looking after and dusting off. They survive between late modernity's premises and projected promises, its gashed and deeply dashed hopes. The migrant, then, is the racially in-visible figure of the postracial moment, its seemingly racially unmarked racial subject.

Hyper-migrations are proliferating globally. They are prompted by the push and pulls of economic intensifications, fading social security, contested nationalist state formations and boundaries, environmental dislocations, racial outbreaks, low-level battles and more intensive wars. Migrants and refugees are no longer so readily distinguishable. On the pull side, demands for labor both within states from less to more industrialized regions and from much less to more economically thriving states have shifted. These movements have been driven also by capital's interests in greater labor flexibility, expanded contingency, and servicing greying populations in established economies; in driving down immediate production expenses, discounting externalities by passing along to the state the costs necessary to secure society; and providing a stable social environment for production and consumption.

The older modernist mode of "going and resting" (Josipovici 1993) is now being displaced by constantly moving and being moved along. Migration traditionally was about becoming rooted for a more or less extended period. Migrancy today concerns being forced to keep on moving. It is about weighing up social and opportunity costs and benefits as work, pressed social and living conditions, and distance from loved ones make eking out an existence more or less bearable. Societies now treat migrants less as a sustaining resource than as temporary hyper-extractive labor, a potential nuisance, moral challenge, burden, or threat. There is little reason in return, consequently, to show social commitment, loyalty, or responsibility.

Migrations are disorienting and dislocating for those arriving, and a challenge to settled inhabitants. This novel migrancy prompts renewed modes of racial articulation, including disparaging characterizations. Migrants are those least advantaged and most vulnerable, targeted as begrudging presence and necessary service by both the socially dominant and the less advantaged. The former tend to express their concerns in terms of racially articulated worries around safety, pollution, and an otherwise slipping quality of life; the more socially disadvantaged voice concerns about their further social erosion in the face of competitively lowered labor and raised rental costs. Race is exercised without having to be explicitly stated.

The elsewheres from which migrants hail today tend to be parts of the planet long racially differentiated from the global North (or from provinces distinguished by their ethno-racially charged economic and cultural poverty). Migrants are hyper-visible, socially badged by a mix of non-belonging markers like language, dress, and implicitly skin color. They are made nevertheless to occupy the hidden corners of the social, more or less invisible in their hyper-visibility, at once seen and unseen: the mall corner awaiting low-wage day-labor opportunities rather than the employment bureau or temporary labor supply office; running drugs rather than grocery stores; trading illicit goods rather than futures. The undocumented stand in momentary fear of police apprehension while readily employed in menial day work or trade, driving uninsured or unlicensed while police turn a blind eye to their lack of legal status. This highly charged invisibility perfectly exemplifies postraciality's winking at its obvious racial invocation in the name of its insistent erasure. Raciality is informally invoked, extended in its deniability. It benefits from its denied orderings and self-distancing from its explicit terms of racial endearment and alienation.

Under conditions marked today as the "postracial," then, we can allegorically summarize its prevailing racial subjections as "walking while black," "enduring as Gazan or Palestinian," and "moving as a migrant." Driving while black was and remains an occupational hazard, most notably but not only in the United States. Walking while black almost anywhere, especially in "white" American landscapes today, however, is an existential hazard. The persistent presence of Palestinians, represented most readily by ghostly and underground Gazan endurance, and the expanding mobility of Muslims increasing their presence globally have posed anew in the name of securitization the challenge to

"Western" societies. They test Western claims to tolerance, built on principles of Christian charity and white privilege. Thirteen percent of Germans today support participating in public demonstrations against Muslim migrants. The demands to supply cheap menial labor while being constantly moved along all but silently renew a political economy of racial articulation under the guise of its erasure.

What the racial of postraciality represents, accordingly, in terms of its proliferating outbreaks, its viralities and skirmishes, is a generalized technology of *informalized* social ordering and management. As demographic and cultural heterogeneity has magnified both actually and virtually in the wake of globalizing and digital forces, states increasingly have shed policies, regulations, and laws explicitly discriminating by race. Race has become less a *formal* technology of state management. Even for state apparatuses like the police, the racial represents individuated responses on the part of particular officers and local departments. Racial expression is invariably dismissed or disciplined as anomalous rather than addressed in explicit policy directives, let alone legally mandated rules and regulations. As the state reaches for generalized mandates across the population, older racial technologies of control have given way to prolific individualized outbursts and surrogate legal terms: institutions can then disavow racial expression, their representatives washing the organization's hands while proclaiming helplessness in the name of free expression to do much if anything about it.

So postraciality represents less that racisms have ended than that state management regarding racist invocation has been transformed. No longer an expressive mandate of the state, racial reference has been purged from state use. Racisms consequently have been informalized. The state simply shapes the conditions of racial possibility on the part of private citizens, institutions, and organizations. In expanding its apparatuses of securitization both internally and externally, the state can simply imply that it is responding to terrorizing violence and criminalization where they occur, inattentive to the racial identification of the perpetrators. In short, postraciality expunges race from state directive, freeing racisms to circulate and proliferate by all other means possible.

In light of these inversions and extensions the question persists: are we all postracial already?

FIVE

Are we all postracial yet?

Postraciality, I have been arguing throughout, rather than expressing the end of racism, conceals within its conceptual erasure of race the driving mode of contemporary racist articulation. Racisms dis-appear behind the formal deletion of racial classification, state regulation, and legal refusal of racial definition. They express themselves anew in the name of racial disappearance, disavowal, and denial. Racisms proliferate in the wake of the supposed death of race.

Postraciality accordingly represents racial re-articulation in the age of contemporary globalization. Globalization magnifies population movements and migrations, intensifying demographic heterogeneity and cultural intersection. Networking culture further shrinks space-time, dramatically narrowing geographical and cultural distance. Yet it simultaneously magnifies distinction, reifying virtual and symbolic distance. It ramifies cultural and political divides, loosens constraints and limitations, licensing prolific racial alienation.

Racial politics in one place influence, interact with, and shore up, in ways large and small, racial politics in other global sites. Racial politics, in any contestation, are often global in scope and interaction, even if they remain stubbornly, emphatically local in design and effect.

Postraciality is "a reality shaped around your own desires," to bend Zadie Smith's (2014) telling words from a different context. "There is something sociopathic," she continues, "in that ambition" of fabricating the world to one's designs. This sociopathy has to do with ordering the world to preclude or delimit not just participation by but the very presence of those deemed not to belong, the racially unfit, undesirable, and unfitting. Richard Cohen's (2014: 173) insistence that Israelis, "by dint of their advanced culture," had a founding right to expel all Palestinians is an especially extreme example of this recently spiraling sociopathy. The enemy, Cohen (2014: 174) continues, "had to go," not as "a case of racism or colonialism but of security based on common sense." Israel, he insists, was fully justified in conducting "ethnic cleansing for a better world" (Weiss 2014). Cohen's denial of Israel's founding racism and colonialism is belied by the very language he invokes: advanced culture, common sense, historical necessity, even ethnic cleansing.

This reveals two key characteristics about racisms implicit in my account thus far. First, the modern state is predicated on racial elimination. And, second, racism restricts society to the present in the name of the past. It forecloses the possibility of future cohabitation.

Raciality's "posts"

It should seem evident that, in key ways, the postracial is to the racial as the postcolonial is to the colonial. It is not the end of racial determination, just as postcoloniality did not signal colonial's end. Rather, it is a different mode by which the racial is lived out. Anne McClintock (1992) remarks that the shift from coloniality to postcoloniality indicates one from relations of power (the colonizer and colonized) to the linearity of time (progress from before to after, worse to better off). This in turn covers over, drawing attention away from, those who continue to benefit and suffer from postcolonial conditions (the "ex-colonizers" and their "casualties").

A similar logic marks the postracial condition too. Racisms reprise at the very moment of racial erasure – only now unmarked, less seen and recognizable. So just as the "post-" in the postcolonial is not the end but the afterlife of the colonial, so too the "post" in postraciality: the afterlife, the ghostly haunting by the racial of the social supposedly rid of the racial. And just as a small group of postcolonial powerbrokers were its overwhelming beneficiaries, so too a distinct minority of the once racially subjugated have been the principal beneficiaries of postracial conditions. To be postracial, just as to be postcolonial, is to imply that the society in question must have been racial (just as it once engaged in colonial practice). But the implication of raciality is not quite an admission, indeed it implies a denial, of its once and present racism. The postracial, then, is racial as a spirit condition of the social, sociality's unnamed because unnameable spirit, its shadow being. The postracial is another modality of racially marked and exclusionary sociality.

The "post" of postraciality reaches for raciality's afterlife. But afterlives come in various forms, relatively hellish or heavenly. I have been arguing that the hellish dominates the heavenly; or more precisely that the supposedly heavenly for some is predicated on making life hellish for others, for those othered, through avoidance and evasion as much as by design and (in)direction.

Anthroporacism signals something of a re-modeled return to the pre-Darwinian conception of races: a form of "species life." After Darwin, human races came to be distinguished in terms of sub-species presumed to be human, if differentially mature. For postraciality, as for pre-Darwinism, the contrast today, at least informally, is between those considering themselves human and those deemed animal, between full members of the human species and those treated as beastly, the lowest of animals. Self-attributing humans reserve for themselves all the virtues of an idealized humanity: humanism, humanitarian aid, the cultured learning a canonical education in the humanities provides, the self-authorization to discipline and the authority to determine who shall live and who shall (be allowed to) die. They reduce the animalized, in turn, to living lives of degradation and desperation in a constantly critical condition.

Relatedly, the "post" of postraciality is not just the mark of the temporal, or the reach for an atemporality, an aspirational time beyond time, a dream state of nonracial being. It is also a post – a stake – in the ground. Here the "post" represents more apprehensively a claim to turf, an assertion of place and power at the expense of those rejected or displaced from the neighborhood or the nation. The "post" here also makes possible widespread display of the flag, rallying around its assertive and symbolic power.

The postracial – raciality's reach for a temporality beyond itself – thus signifies qualities both aspirational and apprehensive. In its most appealing sense, aspiration regarding racial matters concerns the reach for a sociality unbounded by the conceptual and material constraints associated with racial definition. In its more delimiting expression, the aspirational concerns simply the rejection of racial definition, with little transforming impact on historical and existing racial inequities. The latter, I have been insisting, has dominated the driving conception of postraciality. It represents the hardening of demeaning racist expression and the deepening of racially indexed inequities.

The Personal Genome Project (PGP), focusing on generating complete individual genetic data in their environmental interaction, was supposed to silence racial determination once and for all. It would diversify the population at the level of the personal and individual. Genome editing, in turn, personalizes the capacity to address individual genetic challenges. Editing DNA sequencing will eventually make it possible to repair the causes of difficult physical conditions or potentially fatal illnesses, like cystic fibrosis in a newborn. The postraciality inherent in contemporary genetic data gathering is readily on display, nevertheless, in two ways. First, PGP is driven to deploy race in seeking to guarantee diverse population data sets. It seeks out racially defined groupings to guarantee more heterogeneity than the overwhelmingly white males tending to form their principal constituency. Second, prevailing social values shape personal preference schemes, establishing the aesthetic criteria potentially determining what "racial" genes to alter to achieve a better-looking or healthier population. In good post-racial fashion, race is remade through individuation, genomics extending the life of anthroporaciality.

The apprehensive quality associated with postraciality concerns both the worry by the dominant of the loss of their competitive edge and insecurity regarding their accumulated assets. It thus is consistent with, even fueling, the second of the aspirational senses above. But the quality of apprehension attending postraciality hints also at the apprehending, the arresting, character of its object. The arresting is what brings us up short. It projects the desirable but unattainable, threatening possibility, potentially putting a stop to it, curtailing or even ending its capacities. It precludes pathways to futures other than those designated, the socially licensed.

The postracial represents just such designated social conditions. It is above all concerned to restrict to some what it makes available to others. That the restriction is implicitly conditioned on racial terms signals both that the terms are rendered invisible, or at least less visible, and the capacity to deny racist arrangement, expression, or intentionality. However, in extending racially implicated restriction to some, it at least implicitly imposes delimitations on all. As the prevailing raciality of our time, the postracial would have us all marked by the structured inchoateness of race made visibly invisible and invisibly visible. This is the enigmatic quality not just of racism without race but of racisms without racism (Goldberg 2009: 360–3).

So, are we all postracial yet?

The answer will surprise. We indeed are all postracial already. Only not in the conventional sense the question presupposes. It should be obvious from the evidence provided that socio-structurally we remain very much bound by race. So we are hardly postracial in any literal sense. Rather, we are all postracial *structurally* by being drawn into the generalized and now unavoidable social logic of postraciality. This is not to say every person or institution is racist under the sociality of postraciality, least of all anti-racists, just as not everyone or institution was racist under segregation, Jim Crow, or apartheid. It is to say, though, that all those inhabiting subject positions of racial power and domination – notably those who are racially white in its various formulations in different racially articulated societies – project and extend racist socialities by default. But the default is not the only position to occupy or in which to invest. One remains with the default because it is the given, the easiest to inhabit, the sociality of thoughtlessness.

Thoughtlessness

Racisms constitute *thoughtlessness*, in the Arendtian sense of failing to exercise reflective (and by extension self-reflective) critical judgment (Arendt 1963/2006: 234–52). They lack critical and indeed self-critical imagination. They refuse or fail to take account of those racially differentiated as having equal standing, or making valuable contributions. Thoughtless racisms resist attending to the workings of wrongdoing and the racist subject's or society's role in them, unintentional or inadvertent, institutional or structural. Here, racisms are driven by shallowness and carelessness, an ignorant or arrogant refusal to consider conditions beyond one's own and those akin to one. Racisms, it could be said, are narcissisms, nihilizing self-regard, of especially extreme kinds.

There is, to follow Arendt's line, a banality to much racism. It consists in the shocking ordinariness of its everyday occurrences (Essed 1991) and the ordinariness with which its culture of shock (value) has come to be received. More and more, racist expression is reduced to oversight, neglect, a shrug, increasingly the denial not just of racist expression but of the denial itself. What might be called "hot racism," following Billig's (1995: 43–6) analysis of "banal nationalism," is considered characteristic of the outburst exceptions rather than everyday banalities. The shocking quality is buried, alive (Goldberg 2009), beneath the ordinary, everyday, unresisting acceptance of the radical reduction of people to data points in the schedule of instrumental operation. The routinizing instrumentalization of racists represents an unthinking objectification of their human subjects as targets. In a deep sense, racists do not know – or at least not fully – what they do. They may, of course, seek to irk, degrade, or dehumanize. Yet even in those cases they are most likely utterly unthinking about the full dimensions of their actions and their impacts, refusing the implications for all involved.

The logic of "this failure to think," as Judith Butler (2011b) puts it in illuminating Arendt's view, is of a de-moralizing piece in making "thinkable" the likes of drone strikes or demeaning racist jokes to contemporary political purpose. The unthinking of racisms (as opposed to their un-thinking, their undoing or unmaking) renders populations and individual people disposable, nuisances to be set aside or destroyed. Racisms, in

Butler's extended terms, "destroy the very conditions of thinking itself" in undermining critical judgment and ethical consideration underpinning the relation between individual and collective belonging.

So the "popularity" of postracialism, such as it is, has less to do with "completing the civil rights struggle" (Taylor 2012: 23–4) in any idealistic sense than with no longer having to make the sustained effort demanded by the undoing of racisms. It has more to do with assuaging any lingering guilt for racist expression and persistence, and denying structural and institutional articulations of racism. Its appeal is invested in helping to whitewash the license to say privately pretty much anything derogatory about those who are animalized, unconstrained by any material consequences.

Un-thinking racisms

A *thinking* response to racisms, and to postraciality as the prevailing contemporary articulation of the racial, is one that un-thinks – that critically picks apart – the premises on which it is predicated. Here the distinctions between nonracialism, anti-racialism, and anti-racism require attention. *Anti-racialism* seeks to end racial reference. It tends to be a politics from dominance, from power seeking to hang on to its social standing or force, to extend itself. Pushed in isolation as the proper response to racism, it has always entailed no more than erasing the evidence of racisms rather than addressing their structures, deeds, and effects.

The *nonracial* tends even in its grammar to signify a retrospective state of being, always in contrast to the conditions it claims to be negating, if from which it is not quite always completely taking its leave. *Anti-racism*, by comparison, is presentist, active, indeed activist in disposition, rather than passive, and forward-looking in defining "the dream" (Mbembe 2014) of a just state to come. Conceived as a set of dispositions and commitments, anti-racism is a process ongoing in its undertaking. It is not reducible to a singular event. It is not simply "we are the world," Live Aid, or Durban 2001. Nor is it just the United Nations Statements on Race, the Freedom Charter, or the Civil Rights Law, as important as all three have been. It is, at the very least, the abolition, anti-colonial, anti-apartheid, and civil rights *movements* that produced these progressive plateaus in the processes of anti-racist struggle.

Anti-racisms, it follows, require renewed, persistent, historically concretized interventions to push back against racisms' reiterabilities. They require sustaining and extending the benchmarks of critical socialities not stricken by racist structures or outbursts. The work of anti-racism, as is now painfully evident, is not over when we all sing "We Shall Overcome" or "Nkosi Sikelel' iAfrika," when Mandela or Obama are (s)elected, or Palestinians achieve statehood, even one with Israel. Anti-racism requires not just being against the existing and past forms of racist expression, but doing so in the name of an affirming set of ideals – the dream – of what a society not driven by racial consideration in any (consequential) way would look like.

Racial anti-racism thus sometimes requires racial identification both to recognize those targeted by racist orderings and to respond by offsetting the debilitating effects. There is a recognition that, absent deploying race as identifier of the wronged and the appropriate referent for rectification, individually or collectively, the durable conditions of racist arrangement would extend, even deepen, unaddressed. So racial anti-racism might take the form of affirmative action or racially based reparations. Invoking race in such instances is considered necessary to identifying those who have suffered the cumulative legacy of racist injustice over time. Here racial invocation or identification is pragmatic, a somewhat paradoxical or enigmatic means to social life beyond the limiting conditions of the racial.

Historically, *nonracial anti-racisms* have tended to stress individual rights over group rights or claims, emphasizing the *nonracial* rather than anti-racisms. They have tended to elevate concerns about racial definition and characterization over racist subjugation and oppression, debilitation and exclusion, perhaps on the assumption that racial reference inevitably entails racist implications. But there is no inherent necessity to the devolution from racial to racist reference. It remains at least an open question whether racial invocation inherently produces racist inevitability. In any case, the presumption of inevitability is depressingly pessimistic: effectively addressing racisms requires pragmatically taking up their terms of subjugation to push back at, critically address, or redress their impacts. By shying away from the invocation of race for fear that it will inherently encourage the extension of racism, we remain bound by racist inevitability until even descriptive racial reference is socially excised.

Racisms are persistent, even as they morph in kind. They are processes of establishment or revival, persistence and renewal. In contrast to the merely anti-racial, their effective response requires anti-racist commitments equal to the vigor and transitivity of racisms, attendant also to the specificities of their expression. It is worth insisting, against any pessimism (of the intellect), on a more optimistic belief that different contexts require appropriate critical responses specific to the conditions at work. These critical responses build both analytic insight and engaged interventions from coalitions regarding the critical concern at hand. Against the pessimism of anti-racialism, there is a long if varied tradition of commitments to resisting the exploitative and oppressive conditions produced through racial subjugation, best represented, for instance, in the struggles of Black Consciousness. It takes "Black," as Steve Biko (1978) put it, as a matter not of "pigmentation" but of "mental attitude," of critical disposition. This is the first step, he insisted, towards "emancipation" from subjugation and "subservience."

Anti-racisms, as a consequence, tend most effectively to be a politics from below, a critical coalitional politics of insurgency and unsettlement. They can be muddied or unsteady in their grounding, redirected or waylaid by the assumptions of their operationalizing. Anti-racism is usually thought of as undoing or reversing the political economy of racial sovereignty and superiority. Less often there is a call to derail the social ontology and architecture of racial classification, and the social ordering and positioning they establish and sustain, the building blocks of racisms' constitution. If anti-racisms are to be sustainably effective, they must seek more compellingly to undercut the limits of instrumentalizing "thoughtlessness." They must seek more broadly to cultivate thinking, cultures of engaged critique of the histories of racist exclusion and humiliation. Their aim is to undo imposed death and life's foreshortening, disincentive and lack of opportunity for those racially maligned so others are guaranteed advancement.

This suggests a relational distinction between a responsive anti-racism and an ecological one. Responsive anti-racisms are immediate, counter-acting the expressed or eventful racisms of the moment. They tend by nature to be reactive, and are often intended as disruptive. They look to bring up short those engaged in or supporting racist expression either actively or by their silence. Ferguson activists in St Louis exemplified a compelling instance of disruptive anti-racism. Purchasing tickets to an otherwise overwhelmingly white patronage of the St Louis Symphony one Saturday evening, a couple of activists stood up in the audience as the orchestra started the program's second half with Bach's Requiem. The multi-raced anti-racists belted out "Which Side Are You On" as others joined in across the hall and colleagues unfurled banners from the balcony reading "Racism Lives Here" and "Requiem for Michael Brown, 1996–2014." The audience response was a mix of applauding appreciation and appalled incomprehension. The intervention lasted less than five minutes, activists leaving peacefully chanting "Black lives matter!" as they exited (Boggioni 2014). But no one could have departed the evening without giving thought to the point of the intervention.

By an *ecological* anti-racism I mean one responding not simply to immediate racist expressions or events. It seeks to address the larger landscape of structural conditions supporting and enabling the reproduction of racist arrangements and expression. This too was implicit in the symphonic protest. The targets of ecological anti-racisms include the racial status quo marking differentiated racial positions of social, economic, and legal power and status. Ecological anti-racism ranges from critical work uncovering the ongoing structures of racial power to active engagements to transform the structural landscape. The latter involves not simply integrating greater numbers of the racially disprivileged into existing social structures. The point rather is to transform those structures forming the basis of racist degradation to render them more representative of a just polity in a world increasingly constituted by heterogeneous societies. Ecological anti-racisms require sustained coalitional social movements driven by a commitment to broad social principles and ideals.

Anti-racisms call for a refusal of the contemporary rewriting of racial histories to wipe them clean of responsibility (Richard Cohen's [2014] justification of the Nakba being a recent example). They require disordering the racial constitution of worlds and world-making. They call, in addition, for a commitment to heterogenizing not just the imagination but also those who are contributing to the social transformation of the imagined commonplace. This entails depurifying its subject matters and modes of being, proliferating their sites, styles, and subjects of engagement, possibility, and value. Anti-racisms today, then, actively and assertively refuse to take for granted that conditions for which racisms stand are somehow naturalized and ahistorical inevitabilities and irreversibilities. These conditions include the spiraling inheritance of inequality and inequity, of reproduced debilitation and (the threat of) persistent premature death. They involve the deepening oligarchic imbalances of power and wealth, as well as the overlooked inaccessibilities and injustices of the everyday.

Generally, then, anti-racialism is a commitment principally to ending racial reference. Anti-racism, by contrast, undertakes to end the conditions materially and conceptually (re)producing racially predicated injustice. Just as racisms give rise to racial definition, so effective anti-racisms will lead eventually to dissipating racial reference.

Postraciality at best reduces any response to racisms to the reactive. Whether or not we are postracial yet is less the compelling question to pose, then, than to ask what racial work is being effected by the concept of the postracial and the practices in its name. This book offers a sustained response to the latter question.

There is, however, another set of questions to be addressed in closing that are complementary and pressing. How might a society configure itself outside the bounds of the racial while mindful of its debilitating racist histories? And how might people live their lives relationally unrestricted by racial convention and contention, by racisms?

Is it possible to be nonracial in a society historically constituted and continuing as multi-racial, and on what terms? Is there a compelling critical conception of the *nonracial*: the *dream* of a sociality beyond the skin and the surface, as Achille Mbembe (2014) has posed it, and all it is tied up with? Of the nonracial as a set of commitments that, while critical of, are not so narrowly bounded by the histories of race and racisms? Of conditions that enable life after racisms unrestricted by their regulations and constraints?

Can an agile conception of freedom be articulated, one of emancipated life for which race is a history lesson rather than a continuing structuring technology? And can a robust nonraciality be conceived open to, indeed representative of, as wide-ranging lived formations as make up our worlds today? Which is to ask, how do we extend our *un-thinking*, our thinking beyond the limitations of racialities?

Racisms establish, set in place, and extend races, not the reverse. Of course, once established, racial configurations often, though not necessarily, reinforce racisms, reproducing and renewing them. Once established, racial commitments are more readily invoked, especially in social circumstances more pressed and contested around resource availability and its lack, exploitability of labor, access to and restriction of social affordances, and perceived threats to livelihood and security. Racisms are taken up to exercise power in relation to and over others, advance interests, maintain standing and sustain social position while securing a competitive edge. Postraciality is no different.

Insisting on integration is important in advancing equity and social justice in the face of segregated social arrangements. Yet its stress reinforces the presumed discreteness of racial definition. It potentially reinforces the very conditions establishing, renewing, and sustaining the grounds of racial injustice. The problem is less that people commit themselves to ethnoracial identifications and their associated practices than that, as with dogmatic religious profession, they insist that their commitments are the best or only worthy way of being in the world, living a dignified life, and achieving excellence.

Living without postraciality

In asking how to un-think racial configuration, we are seeking ways of living outside its determinations. Living outside racial determination, in turn, means being both unbound by its holds and reparative of its historical inequities and injustices without at once reinstating, rearranging, or renewing them. Racial commitments tend to insist on social homogeneity and the privilege, if not social purity, of naturalized kinship relations. A recent study revealed that 73 percent of whites surveyed "rated whites significantly higher than other ethnic groups as best representing America." Only 27 percent considered blacks, Asians, Latinos, and white Americans "as equally representative of American values and ideals" (Danbold and Huo 2014). A just sociality unbounded by the racial would be predicated upon recognizing the appeal of heterogeneous aesthetic and cultural values and expression, in ways of being and doing, in modes of world-making. It would map out social relations absent racial domination. Openness to heterogeneity and its social practices requires cultivation as disposition, as outlook on life.

The most compelling examples of anti-racist movements tend to be driven by coalitional engagements of activists, artists, intellectuals, and others committed to a social vision and practice of critical nonracial engagement. They seek to turn responses to racist moments into sustained anti-racist movements. These movements are mindful about not reinstating racial hierarchies of power and decision-making parading behind the rhetoric of the nonracial. Examples include nineteenth-century abolitionism, the mid-twentieth-century civil rights struggle and anti-apartheid movements, and Rock Against Racism in Britain in the 1970s. Contemporarily, important networks include Critical Resistance (the US prison abolitionist initiative), the gathering Zwarte Piet youth campaign in the Netherlands today as well as the broader coalition against Dutch racism (Essed and Hoving 2014), involving among others the "Reason Against Racism" Facebook Collective (2014) and the New Urban Collective. The growing US campaign against deadly policing practices, and the Boycott,

Divestment, Sanctions (BDS) movement concerning Israel/Palestine, are similarly important. All have at least some global dimension to them. They require resourcefulness and resilience to sustain them through the inevitable rough patches of disinterest and repression. They call for work-arounds and make-overs, strategic and tactical thinking about interventions, disruptions, and provocations. The Ferguson anti-racists seeking to unsettle the St Louis social elite in the symphonic silences reproducing their confirmatory and conforming whiteness offer one instance.

From effective examples of coalitional anti-racist movements, principles of critical engagement can be teased out. The Freedom Charter in South Africa (Congress Alliance 1955) offers an exemplary critical anti-racism in the form of a seemingly enigmatic racial nonracialism. Its circumstances of engagement, explicitly situated and historically specific, nevertheless can be generalized sufficiently to offer compelling history lessons. It sought to address the legacy of debilitating, destructive, and deadly racisms by outlining a set of commitments informing the framing of the progressive new South African constitution in the mid-1990s. And it continued to hold out a set of premises and promises in the face of the country's contemporary slippages, denials, and refusals.

The Freedom Charter spells out in summary form a set of constituting principles underpinning a just society as counter to the formalizing apartheid of its day. Marking the driving principles is a baseline commitment that the rights and benefits of the society should apply, equally, to all irrespective of racial identification. These driving principles include equal rights for all, equal protection of the law, the fair sharing of the country's wealth and land, freedom of speech and association, the right to vote, freedom of movement and occupation, equal pay for equal work, access to equal education and resources necessary to a healthy, dignified life of well-being for all. No proponent of postraciality comes close to endorsing this range of rights.

It is crucial to note here that ongoing acknowledgment of the social existence of racial groupings is considered instrumentally key in the given circumstances to securing equal rights nonracially recognized and sustaining the possibility of dignified, respected, and flourishing lives for all. Postraciality seeks artificially to erase race from social reference schemes and vernaculars. By contrast, the Freedom Charter recognizes the persistence of racial reference and characterization in a society deeply marked by race historically. It proceeds not by insisting that race have no place in social reference in a polity long ordered by it. Rather, it insists on equality for all in the face of ongoing racial reference irrespective of any official call for its erasure. The institution of equal rights substantively will likely lead to the fading of any material reason for racial reference. The point is not to push it underground, where its dirty work can extend unaddressed. In characterizing blackness not as skin color but as a consciousness committed to resisting black subservience, Biko's "Black Consciousness" (1978: 48–53) similarly advances blackness less as an inherent racial designation than as a category of political organizing in the face and wake of racisms and their legacies.

Crucial here is a pragmatic commitment to a critical racialism and a structural anti-racism. In holding out nonracialism as an ideal horizon for which to strive, both the Freedom Charter and Black Consciousness signal human becoming and possibility equal to whites for those denied them in racist societies. The nonracial here punctures racist socialities both in conception and in practice. It offers a vision of a counter-sociality for which to struggle in the name of which racial boundaries are (to be) transgressed.

Founded in 1982, the Rainbow Restaurant and Jazz Club in Pinetown, a now largely Zulu neighborhood of Durban, was inspired from the outset by the Freedom Charter's anti-apartheid and critical nonraciality. Even in the most repressive days of 1980s apartheid, the club, led by the inimitable Ben Pretorius, insisted on racially mixed acts and audiences, the site of lived opposition to segregation in the face of persistent persecution, security police visits, threats of license suspension, and arrests. It remains today a site of experimentation and openness, heterogeneity and inter-racial conviviality. It represents what I would call an *experiential* nonracialism and anti-racism in contrast to structural ones, as ownership, management, and overall control have always remained in the hands of whites. As important as experiential anti- and nonracialisms are as modes of resistance even to *institutional* racisms, the latter cannot be effectively undone in the final analysis until their larger structural conditions are likewise critically transformed.

The Rainbow Restaurant and the Freedom Charter, popularized through a widespread national signing campaign in 1955–6, exemplify the politics of protests and public space, including the street. Street protests and the club as both site and expression of protest not only establish the publicness of gathering spaces, as Judith Butler (2011a) has helpfully argued. Their gathering eventfulness, whether episodic or serial, establishes both a counter-raciality and, more often than not, a critical nonraciality. They model for society what inter-, trans-, alter- and indeed nonraciality would amount to if fully institutionalized. They often offer, also, animating symbols as the gathering battle-cry for critical resistance: the Black Power and "Amandla" fists, the toyi-toyi dance, and, revealingly perhaps today, "Hands Up, Don't Shoot," "I Can't Breathe," and "Black Lives Matter." Mississippi's Freedom Summer (1964) and the nonracial coalition to save the Sea Point Pavilion swimming pool in Cape Town from commercial development (2008) similarly represent in their counters compelling exemplifications of life between and beyond the color line.

The Sea Point experiment is especially revealing. The Pavilion is one of the world's most beautifully placed outdoor swimming pools. It juts out into the Atlantic under the majestic shadows of Lion's Head and Table Mountain behind it, looking across the bay at Robben Island. Until apartheid ended it was reserved exclusively for white use, "Coloureds" tending to the pool's upkeep. (Full disclosure: I learned to swim in the junior pool.) Under post-apartheid, the pool has become the site of Cape Town's most mixed-race convivial recreationality, cutting deeply across the city's articulation of race, class, gender, and religion. Scarfed Muslim women picnic aside near-naked men and women of all colors and convictions. The campaign to save the pool from commercial development deepened the inter-racial social relations and engagement already in place (Verster 2008). It links anti-racism to a critique of rampant capitalism. It models more effectively than most examples what the dream and practice of a nonracial sociality could amount to and to which we should aspire.

Postraciality, on the terms I have insisted upon, got Trayvon Martin and Michael Brown killed, among a growing number of other young black people in America. Anti-racism reveals the structural conditions underpinning residential segregation, seeking to address their causal factors. Its relative success would render it commensurately less likely that Martin would have seemed out of place and Brown would have been the resident of a segregated black-only neighborhood. To the extent that a critical nonracial society is constituted, neither Brown nor Martin would have been apprehended because vigilante or police suspiciousness would not have been directed at them in virtue of their blackness. Absent racist social arrangements and presumptuous white social agents, they would likely both be alive today.

Racisms demean, degrade, humiliate. They render their targets always less than they are, opening the way to their violent treatment by individuals, the state and its agents. They also distort the perpetrators.

179

The pressing question now, in any society still stricken by debilitating raciality, is not whether we are all postracial yet. Societies today are increasingly heterogeneous, marked more and more by global flows and their traces. A society can only restrain such heterogeneity by the sorts of repression and closure long delivered by racial articulation and social militarization. The horizon of the nonracial is represented by the reach for societies outside, beyond, and ungoverned by any restraining and restricting bounds of race. A society unlimited by race, actually and virtually, is achievable only in concert, individually, across groups, globally. It is achievable in the end only by becoming fully free.

Postraciality is the illusion that the dream of the nonracial has already been realized. The task of thinking beyond race, however, is to lay out a social vision creatively and ethically worthy of all society's heterogeneous inhabitants. It is to un-think contemporary incapacitations and limits on the possibilities of societies privileging some at the cost to most. It is not that one has to be fellow travelers on the bus, so much as freedom riders jamming with, riffing off, playing with and pushing back reiteratively, reformingly, and renewingly against the ideas and practices that sustain lives aside and against socialities of the skin.

180

Using all means necessary, from street to screen, the dream of nonraciality is to fashion globally open societies in creative and critical engagement with others without turning them into the Other. The suffocation of racist sociality is to be replaced with a social atmosphere in which all can breathe free. The drive, in short, is to remain persistently anti-racist while sustainably living together without the walls and weapons of the (post)racial.

Abramovich, Alex 2009. "Phenomenologically fucked," *London Review of Books*, 31, 22 (Nov. 19). *http://www.lrb.co.uk/v31/n22/alex-abramovich/phenomenologically-fucked*

Abu El-Haj, Nadia 2012. *The Genealogical Science: The Search for Jewish Origins and the Politics of Epistemology*. University of Chicago Press.

Agorist, Matt 2014. "New York Man Detained, Choked and Thrown to the Ground by NYPD – For Dancing in the Street," *The Free Thought Project.com*, December 29. *http://thefreethoughtproject.com/york-man-detained-choked-thrown-ground-nypd-dancing-street/*

Ahmed, Sara 2014a. "Brick Walls: Racism and Other Hard Histories," 14th Annual Critical Race and Postcolonial Studies Conference, October 18. *http://www.criticalracenetwork.com/conference-2014/conference-program/keynote-speakers*

Ahmed, Sarah 2014b. "White Men," *feministkilljoys*, November 4. *http://feministkilljoys.com/2014/11/04/white-men/comment-page-1/#comment-5632*

Alter, Charles 2014. "Watch a Police Officer Stop a Michigan Man with His Hands in his Pockets," December 1. *http://time.com/3611812/pontiac-police-michigan-stop-man-hands-pockets-cold/*

Amin, Ash 2010. "The Remainders of Race," *Theory, Culture & Society*, 27, 1: 1–23. *http://tcs.sagepub.com/content/27/1/1*

Anonymous 2014. "If Anyone missed this: #Police Chief Tim Fitch Studies Counter-Terrorism in Israel with the IDF," *Twitter*, August 15. *https://twitter.com/YourAnonNews/status/499762962077196288*

Araújo, Joel Zito 2014. *Raça (Race): Um Filme sobre a Igualdade.* *http://www.racafilme.com/index_english.html*

Arendt, Hannah 1963/2006. *Eichmann in Jerusalem.* Penguin.

ARRSE 2014. "Israel Ground Invasion of Gaza Has Begun," *Army Rumor Service*, July 17. *http://www.arrse.co.uk/community/threads/israel-ground-invasion-of-gaza-has-begun.216543/page-151*

Auster, Lawrence 2008. "What is Post-Racial America?" *View From the Right*, February 25. *http://www.amnation.com/vfr/archives/010000.html*

Balko, Randy 2013. *Rise of the Warrior Cop: The Militarization of America's Police Forces.* Public Affairs.

Bear, Shalom 2012. "Did Ha'aretz Turn Eli Yishai into a 'Racist' White Man?" *The Jewish Press*, June 25. *http://www.jewishpress.com/news/breaking-news/did-haaretz-turn-eli-yishai-into-a-racist-white-man/2012/06/25/*

Beinin, Joel 2014. "Racism is the Foundation of Israel's Operation Protective Edge," *Jadaliyya*, July 30. *http://www.jadaliyya.com/pages/index/18732/racism-is-the-foundation-of-israels-operation-prot*

Benjamin, Walter 2002. *The Arcades Project.* Harvard University Press.

Biko, Steve 1978. *I Write What I Like, Selected Writings.* University of Chicago Press.

Billig, Michael 1995. *Banal Nationalism.* Sage.

Bittner, Jochen 2014. "What's Behind Germany's New Anti-Semitism," *The New York Times*, September 16. *http://www.nytimes.com/2014/09/17/opinion/jochen-bittner-whats-behind-germanys-new-anti-semitism.html?_r=0*

Boggioni, Tom 2014. "Ferguson Flash Mob Interrupts St Louis Symphony with Requiem for Michael Brown," *RawStory*, October 5.

http://www.rawstory.com/rs/2014/10/watch-ferguson-flash-mob-interrupts-st-louis-symphony-with-requiem-for-michael-brown/

Bonilla-Silva, Eduardo 2003. *Racism without Racists: Colorblind Racism and the Persistence of Racial Inequality in the United States.* Rowman and Littlefield.

Bouie, Jamelle 2014 "Why Do Millennials Not Understand Racism?" *Slate*, May 14. *http://www.slate.com/articles/news_and_politics/politics/2014/05/millennials_racism_and_mtv_poll_young_people_are_confused_about_bias_prejudice.html*

Brooks, Cornell Williams 2014. "Law Enforcement vs Black and Brown Americans," *The New York Daily News*, August 6. *http://www.nydailynews.com/opinion/law-enforcement-black-brown-americans-article-1.1893031*

Brown, Simone 2014. *Dark Matters.* Duke University Press.

Butler, Judith 2011a. "Bodies in Alliance and the Politics of the Street," *Transversal Texts*, September. *http://www.eipcp.net/transversal/1011/butler/en*

Butler, Judith 2011b. "Hannah Arendt's Challenge to Adolf Eichmann," *Guardian*, August 29. *http://www.theguardian.com/commentisfree/2011/aug/29/hannah-arendt-adolf-eichmann-banality-of-evil*

Cain, Herman 2014. Interview on Fox News, December 6. *http://video.foxnews.com/v/3927420215001/herman-cain-reacts-to-ferguson-garner-grand-jury-decisions/#sp=show-clips*

Chait, Jonathan 2014. "The Color of His Presidency," *New York Magazine*, April 6. *http://nymag.com/news/features/obama-presidency-race-2014-4/*

Cheung, Paul 2014. "AAJA Seeks Apology from Fox News for Irresponsible Comments About Islam," *Asian American Journalists Association*, August 27. *http://www.aaja.org/fox-news-islamophobic/*

Chiles, Nick 2013. "Israel Admits 'Shameful' Birth Control Drug Injected in Unaware Ethiopian Jews," *Atlanta Blackstar*, January 29.

References

http://atlantablackstar.com/2013/01/29/israel-acknowledges-shameful-contraceptive-shots-given-to-ethiopian-jews/

Cohen, Richard 2014. *Israel: Is It Good for the Jews?* Simon and Schuster.

Congress Alliance 1955. The Freedom Charter. Kliptown, June 26. *African National Congress. http://www.anc.org.za/show.php?id=72*

Cyran, Olivier 2013. " 'Charlie Hebdo,' Not Racist? If You Say So…" *Article 11*, December 5. *http://posthypnotic.randomstatic.net/charliehebdo/Charlie_Hebdo_article%2011.htm*

Danbold, Felix and Huo, Yuen J. 2014. "No Longer 'All-American'? Whites' Defensive Reactions to Their Numerical Decline," *Social Psychological and Personality Science*, August 19. *http://spp.sagepub.com/content/early/2014/08/13/1948550614546355*

David, M.B. 2014. "Study Finds White Americans Believe They Experience More Racism Than African Americans," *Political Blind Spot*, January 3. *http://politicalblindspot.com/study-finds-white-americans-believe-they-experience-more-racism-than-african-americans/*

Davids, M. Fakhry 2011. *Internal Racism: A Psychoanalytic Approach to Race and Difference*. Palgrave Macmillan.

Demmers, Jolle and Mehendale, Sameer 2010. "Neoliberal Xenophobia in the Netherlands: Construction of an Enemy," *The Populist Imagination 20. http://www.skor.nl/_files/Files/OPEN20_P50-59.pdf*

Derrida, Jacques 2011. *The Beast and the Sovereign*, Volumes I and II. University of Chicago Press.

Diab, Moe 2014. "Israelis Chant 'N*ggers Go Home' Carrying ISIS-Style Flags at Anti-African Rally," *Addicting Info*, October 7. *http://www.addictinginfo.org/2014/10/07/video-israelis-chant-nggers-go-home-carrying-isis-style-flags-at-anti-african-rally/*

Dick, Philip K. 1954/1992. "The Adjustment Team," in *The Collected Stories of Philip K. Dick*. Volume II. Carol Publishing.

References

D'Souza, Dinesh 1996. *The End of Racism: Principles for a Multicultural Society*. Free Press.

D'Souza, Dinesh 2011. *The Roots of Obama's Rage*. Regnery Publishing.

Dyer, Richard 1988. "White," *Screen*, 29, 4 (Autumn): 44–65.

Dyer, Richard 1997. *White: Essays on Race and Culture*. Routledge.

Edwards, Stassa 2014. "From Miasma to Ebola: The History of Racist Moral Panic Over Disease," *Jezebel*, October 14. *http://jezebel.com/from-miasma-to-ebola-the-history-of-racist-moral-panic-1645711030*

Ellison, Ralph 1952. *Invisible Man*. Random House.

Esposito, Roberto 2008 *BIOS: Biopolitics and Philosophy (Posthumanities)*. University of Minnesota Press.

Essed, Philomena 1991. *Understanding Everyday Racism*. Sage.

Essed Philomena 2013. "Entitlement Racism: License to Humiliate," in *Recycling Hatred: Racism(s) in Europe Today*, pp. 62–77. ENAR.

Essed, Philomena and Hoving, Isobel, eds 2014. *Dutch Racism*. Rodopi.

Fang, Marina 2014. "Steve King: Ferguson Protestors are of a 'Continental Origin' So Racial Profiling Is Not a Factor," *Huffington Post*, August 14. *http://www.huffingtonpost.com/2014/08/14/steve-king-ferguson_n_5678677.html*

Fanon, Frantz 1968. *Black Skin, White Masks*. Paladin.

Fausset, Richard 2014. "Mostly Black Cities, Mostly White City Halls," *New York Times*, September 28. *http://www.nytimes.com/2014/09/29/us/mostly-black-cities-mostly-white-city-halls.html?_r=0*

Foucault, Michel 2003. *Society Must Be Defended: Lectures at the Collège de France, 1975–6*. Picador.

Foucault, Michel 2008. *The Birth of Biopolitics: Lectures at the Collège de France 1978–9*. Palgrave Macmillan.

Fullwiley, Duana 2011. *The Encultured Gene: Sickle Cell Heath Politics and Biological Difference in West Africa*. Princeton University Press.

References

Garcia, Ahiza 2014. "Missouri Councilman Explains Racist Facebook Posts: 'I was a Very Active Republican," *TPM*, August 20. *http:// talkingpointsmemo.com/livewire/peter-tinsley-obama-facebook-posts*

Gilmore, Ruth Wilson 2007. *Golden Gulag: Prisons, Surplus, Crisis and Opposition in Globalizing California*. University of California Press.

Gilroy, Paul 2010. *Darker than Blue: On the Moral Economies of Black Atlantic Culture (the W.E.B. du Bois Lectures)*. Harvard University Press.

Ginsburg, Justice Ruth Bader 2014. *Vesey et al. v. Perry, Governor of Texas*, dissenting, US Supreme Court 574 US. *http://www. supremecourt.gov/opinions/14pdf/14a393_08m1.pdf*

Goldberg, David Theo 2002. *The Racial State*. Blackwell.

Goldberg, David Theo 2009. *The Threat of Race: Reflections on Racial Neoliberalism*. Wiley-Blackwell.

Goldberg, David Theo 2012. "When Race Disappears," *Comparative American Studies*, 2/3: 116–27.

Goldberg, David Theo 2013. "Enclosure/Disclosure: Writing on the Wall," *Rassegna Italiana di Sociologica* (Milan), July–September: 471–86. *http://www.rivisteweb.it/doi/10.1423/74753*

Goldberg, David Theo and Giroux, Susan 2014. *Sites of Race*. Polity.

Graham, David A. 2014. "Rumsfled's Knowns and Unknowns: The Intellectual History of a Quote," *Atlantic Monthly*, March 27. *http:// www.theatlantic.com/politics/archive/2014/03/rumsfelds-knowns- and-unknowns-the-intellectual-history-of-a-quip/359719/*

Greenwald, Glenn 2014. "The Militarization of US Police: Finally Dragged into the Light by the Horrors of Ferguson," *The Intercept*, August 14. *https://firstlook.org/theintercept/2014/08/14/ militarization-u-s-police-dragged-light-horrors-ferguson/*

Gunaratnam, Jasmin and Murji, Karim 2013. "3D Racism – Denials, Disclaimers and Doubt," *Media Diversified*, November 25. *http://*

References

mediadiversified.org/2013/11/25/3d-racism-denial-disclaimers-and-doubt/

Hage, Ghassan, 2014. "Recalling Anti-Racism," *Mail and Guardian*, August 4. *http://mg.co.za/article/2014-08-04-recalling-anti-racism*

Hall, Stuart 2011. "The Neoliberal Revolution: Thatcher, Blair, Cameron – the Long March of Neoliberalism Continues," *Soundings*, 9–27. *https://www.questia.com/magazine/1P3-2434141461/the-neoliberal-revolution*

Hatmaker, Taylor 2014 "Palestinians Teach Ferguson Protestors How to Deal with Tear Gas," *The Daily Dot*, August 14. *http://www.dailydot.com/politics/ferguson-protest-palestinians-gaza-tear-gas/*

Hollinger, David 2011. "The Concept of Post-Racial: How Its Easy Dismissal Obscures Important Questions," *Daedalus*, 140, 1: 174–82.

Hudson, Adam 2013 "A Black Man Is Killed in the US Every 28 Hours by Police," *Occupy.com*, May 31. *http://www.occupy.com/article/black-man-killed-us-every-28-hours-police*

Immoral Minority 2014 "Xenophobe Rep. Steve King (R-Iowa) is Confronted by Two Dreamers..." August 6. *http://theimmoralminority.blogspot.com/2014/08/xenophobe-rep-steve-king-r-iowa-is.html*

Ioffe, Julia 2014. "White St Louis Has Some Awful Things to Say About Ferguson," *New Republic*, August 15. *http://www.newrepublic.com/article/119102/what-white-st-louis-thinks-about-ferguson*

James, Andre C. 2011. "Uproar Over Facebook Picture Showing Dead Black Boy," *Digital Journal*, August 29. *http://www.digitaljournal.com/article/310899#ixzz1YXO9ekiY*

Josipovici, Gabriel 1993. "Going and Resting," in *Jewish Identity*, eds Michael Krausz and David Theo Goldberg, pp. 309–21. Temple University Press.

References

Khalek, Rianna 2014. "Israeli-Trained Police 'Occupy' Missouri After Killing of Black Youth," *The Electronic Intifada*, August 15. *http://electronicintifada.net/blogs/rania-khalek/israel-trained-police-occupy-missouri-after-killing-black-youth*

Kurtzleben, Danielle 2014. "White High School Dropouts are Wealthier than Black or Latino College Graduates," *Vox*, October 5. *http://www.vox.com/2014/9/24/6840037/white-high-school-dropouts-have-more-wealth-than-black-and-hispanic*

Latour, Bruno 2009. "Perspectivism: 'Type' or 'Bomb,' " *Anthropology Today*, 25, 2 (April): 1–2. *http://www.bruno-latour.fr/sites/default/files/P-141-DESCOLA-VIVEIROSpdf.pdf*

Latour, Bruno 2014. "Agency at the Time of the Anthropocene," *New Literary History*, 45: 1–18. *http://www.bruno-latour.fr/sites/default/files/128-FELSKI-HOLBERG-NLH-FINAL.pdf*

Lee, Jeah 2014. "Exactly How Often do Police Shoot Unarmed Men?" *Mother Jones*, August 15. *http://m.motherjones.com/politics/2014/08/police-shootings-michael-brown-ferguson-black-men*

Levine, Sam 2014. "GOP Congressman Accuses Democrats of 'Waging War on Whites'," *Huffington Post*, August 4. *http://www.huffingtonpost.com/2014/08/04/mo-brooks-war-on-whites_n_5647967.html*

Levinson, David 2014. " 'I am Not Your Brother' – St Paul Cops Allegedly Taser and Arrest Black Male for Sitting in Public Space (Video)," *streets.mn*, August 28. *http://streets.mn/2014/08/28/i-am-not-your-brother-st-paul-cops-allegedly-taser-and-arrest-black-male-for-sitting-in-public-space-video/*

Lipsitz, George 2012. "Beyond Race: An Analysis of Colorblindness in America," *Postracial America*, April 25. *http://postracialamerica.wordpress.com/2012/04/25/beyond-race-an-analysis-of-colorblindness-in-america/#more-75*

McClintock, Anne 1992. "The Angel of Progress: Pitfalls of the Term 'Post-Colonialism,' " *Social Text*, 31/32: 84–98.

References

MacMunn, George Fletcher 1933. *The Martial Races of India*. Mittal Publications.

McWhorter, John 2008 "Racism in America Is Over," *Forbes*, December 30. *http://www.forbes.com/2008/12/30/end-of-racism-oped-cx_jm_1230mcwhorter.html*

McWhorter, John 2010 "It's Official: America is 'Post-Racial' in the Age of Obama," *thegrio.com*. 14 January. *http://thegrio.com/2010/01/14/its-official-america-is-postracial-in-the-age-of-obama/*

Makdisi, Saree 2010. "The Architecture of Erasure," *Critical Inquiry*, 36, 3 (Spring): 519–59.

Mavhunga, Clapperton Chakanetsa 2011, "Vermin Beings: On Pestiferous Animals and Human Game," *Social Text 106*, 29, 1 (Spring): 151–76.

Mazza, Ed 2014. "Russians Mock Obama with Racist Laser Projection on Former US Embassy in Moscow," *The Huffington Post*, August 7. *http://www.huffingtonpost.com/2014/08/06/russia-racist-laser-obama_n_5656732.html*

Mbembe, Achille 2014. "Raceless Futures in Critical Black Thought," *Archives of the Nonracial*, June 29. *http://bog2014.dev.uchri.org/sect/videos/*

Mitchell, W.J.T. 2012. *Seeing Through Race*. Harvard University Press.

Morse, Jack 2014. "Bros Attempt to Kick Kids off Mission Soccer Field," *Uptown Almanac*, October 9. *http://uptownalmanac.com/2014/10/bros-try-kick-kids-soccer-field*

MTV 2014. "Look Different" Survey. *http://www.lookdifferent.org/about-us/research-studies/1-2014-mtv-david-binder-research-study*

Mullen, Jethro and Wedeman, Ben 2014. "'They Went to the Beach to Play': Deaths of 4 Children Add to Growing Toll in Gaza Conflict," *CNN*, July 17. *http://edition.cnn.com/2014/07/17/world/meast/mideast-conflict-children/*

References

Murdock, Sebastian 2014. "Ray Albers, Cop Who Threatened Ferguson Protestors, Resigns," *Huffington Post*, August 29. *http://www. huffingtonpost.com/2014/08/29/ray-albers-fired-ferguson_n_ 5737822.html*

Norton, Michael I. and Sommers, Samuel 2011. "Whites See Racism as a Zero-Sum Game That They Are Now Losing," *Perspectives on Psychological Science*, 6: 215–18. *http://ase.tufts.edu/psychology/ sommerslab/documents/raceInterNortonSommers2011.pdf*

Pew 2014 ."Stark Racial Divisions in Reactions to Ferguson Police Shooting," *Pew Research Center for the People and the Press*, August 18. *http://www.people-press.org/2014/08/18/stark-racial-divisions-in- reactions-to-ferguson-police-shooting/*

Rankine, Claudia 2014. *Citizen: An American Odyssey*. Graywolf Press.

Reason Against Racism Facebook Collective 2014. *https://www.face book.com/groups/Reason2/*

Roithmayr, Daria 2014. *Reproducing Racism: How Everyday Choices Lock in White Advantage*. New York University Press.

Rose, Jacqueline 2005. *The Question of Zion*. Princeton University Press.

Sambrook, Clare 2014. "The Racist Texts: What the Mubenga Trial was not Told," *Our Kingdom*, December 17. *https://www.open democracy.net/ourkingdom/clare-sambrook/racist-texts-what-mubenga- trial-jury-was-not-told*

Sand, Shlomo 2015. "A Fetid Wind of Racism Hovers Over Europe," *CounterPunch*, January 16–18. *http://www.counterpunch.org/ 2015/01/16/je-suis-charlie-chaplin/*

Sargent, Greg 2011 "What Coburn Really Said About Obama, Race, and Dependency," *The Plum Line*, August 18. *http://www. washingtonpost.com/blogs/plum-line/post/what-coburn-really-said- about-obama-race-and-dependency/2011/03/03/gIQAdBywNJ_blog. html*

References

Scott, Dylan 2014. "D'Souza's Ex-Wife Urged the Judge to Throw the Book at Him. He's an Abusive Liar!" *TPM*, September 26. *http://talkingpointsmemo.com/dc/dinesh-dsouza-ex-wife-court-document*

Sharp, Diamond 2014. "White Mother Sues Sperm Bank After Birth of Mixed-Race Daughter," *The Root*, October 1. *http://www.theroot.com/articles/culture/2014/10/white_mother_sues_sperm_bank_after_birth_of_mix_raced_daughter.html*

Siddiqui, Sabrina 2014. "Americans' Attitudes Towards Arabs and Muslims Worsens, Poll Finds," *Huffington Post*, July 29. *http://www.huffingtonpost.com/2014/07/29/arab-muslim-poll_n_5628919.html*

Smith, Zadie 2014. "Find Your Beach," *The New York Review of Books*, October 23. *http://www.nybooks.com/articles/archives/2014/oct/23/find-your-beach/*

Starkey, David 2011. "Racist" David Starkey on England Riots: The Whites Have Become Black. *https://www.youtube.com/watch?v=GLhyYYBIC9k*

Steele, Shelby 2007. *A Bound Man: Why We Are Excited About Obama, and Why He Can't Win*. Free Press.

Steele, Shelby 2008. "Obama's Postracial Promise," *Los Angeles Times*, November 5. *http://www.latimes.com/news/opinion/opinionla/la-oe-steele5-2008nov05-story.html#page=1*

Streets, Heather 2004 *Martial Races: The Military, Race and Masculinity in British Imperial Culture, 1857–1914*. Manchester University Press.

Swart, Werner 2011. "Wanted: Facebook Racist," *Sunday Times* (Johannesburg), August 28. *http://www.timeslive.co.za/local/2011/08/28/wanted-facebook-racist*

Taylor, Paul 2012. "Taking Post-Racialism Seriously: From Movement Mythology to Racial Formation," *http://ptw.uchicago.edu/Taylor13.pdf*

Telles, Edward 2014. *Pigmentocracies: Ethnicity, Race, and Color in Latin America*. University of North Carolina Press.

References

Tesler, Michael and Sears, David 2010. *Obama's Race: The 2008 Election and the Dream of a Post-Racial America*. University of Chicago Press.

Thompson, Derek 2013 "The 33 Whitest Jobs in America," *The Atlantic Monthly*, November 6. *http://www.theatlantic. com/business/archive/2013/11/the-33-whitest-jobs-in-america/ 281180/*

Valayden, Chandiren 2013. Outbreak Racism: The Embrace of Risk after Structural Racism. Dissertation. University of California Irvine.

Verster, François 2008. *Sea Point Days*. Trigon-film. *https://www. trigon-film.org/en/movies/Sea_Point_Days*

Viveiros de Castro, Eduardo 2012 "Culture: The Universal Animal," *Hau Journal*, 1. *http://www.haujournal.org/index.php/masterclass/ article/view/107/135*

Wacquant, Loïc 2009 *Punishing the Poor: The Neoliberal Government of Social Insecurity*. Duke University Press.

Weiss, Philip 2014 " 'Ethnic Cleansing for a Better World' – Richard Cohen Says the Palestinians Brought the Nakba on Themselves," *Mondoweiss*, October 1. *http://mondoweiss.net/2014/10/cleansing-palestinians-themselves*

Wilkie, Christina 2014. "Rick Perry: Record-High Arrests of Migrants from Countries with 'Terrorist Ties,' " *Huffington Post*, August 4. *http://www.huffingtonpost.com/2014/08/03/rick-perry-terrorists_n_ 5645754.html*

Wiltz, Teresa 2014. "Poverty is Rapidly Increasing in Suburbs Like Ferguson," *Huffington Post*, August 26. *http://www.huffingtonpost. com/2014/08/26/ferguson-poverty_n_5716593.html*

Wise, Tim 2009. *Between Barack and a Hard Place: Racism and White Denial in the Age of Obama*. City Lights.

Wise, Tim 2010. *Color-Blindness: The Rise of Post-Racial Politics and the Retreat from Equity*. City Lights.

References

Wisnewski, J. Jeremy. 2010 *30 Rock and Philosophy: We Want to Go to There*. Wiley.

Wray, Diana 2014. "10 Crazy Things in Texas' Proposed New Social Studies Textbooks," *Houston Press*, September 12. *http://blogs. houstonpress.com/news/2014/09/5_crazy_things_in_texas_proposed_ new_social_studies_textbooks.php*

Yardley, Jim 2014. "Europe's Anti-Semitism Comes Out of the Shadows," *New York Times*, September 23. *http://www.nytimes. com/2014/09/24/world/europe/europes-anti-semitism-comes-out-of- shadows.html?_r=0*

Yishai, Eli 2012, "Interview with *Maariv*," June 3 (in Hebrew). *http:// www.nrg.co.il/online/1/ART2/373/346.html*

Your Black World 2014. "Evaluators Find More Errors When They Think the Writer is Black," *yourblackworld.net*, April. *http://www. yourblackworld.net/2014/04/black-news/evaluators-find-more-errors- when-they-think-the-writer-is-black*

195

Index

Index

Index